THE LOOM BOOK

By
Tim Reed
Illustrated by the Author

CHARLES SCRIBNER'S SONS • NEW YORK

Acknowledgments
I am grateful to Allen Parrott and Mary Schultz for allowing
me to investigate their looms.

First published by The Sunstone Press P.O. Box 2321,
Santa Fe, New Mexico 87501

1 3 5 7 9 11 13 15 17 19 M/P 20 18 16 14 12 10 8 6 4 2

Printed in the United States of America
Library of Congress Catalog Card Number 76-48388
ISBN 0-684-14073-X

Photo by Beverly Gile

BIOGRAPHY

Tim Reed, architectural designer, cab driver, carpenter, sculptor, handyman, is rapidly building a reputation in the Southwest for his quality, handmade looms, most of which he designed himself.

Innovations, such as the ratchet system specifically designed for the loom described in this manual, seem native to Reed. As a three-year-old in 1946, he was busy building everything from airplanes to boats from clay, indigenous to his native Santa Fe, New Mexico. This early trait developed naturally and has exhibited itself in forms ranging from rockets made of tin foil and scotch tape to basketball arenas, scrap iron sculptures, rectories, fishing, and Indian village dioramas, looms and on and on.

Reed was graduated from the University of New Mexico at Albuquerque in 1967 with a BA in architecture. He worked for an architectural firm while attending school and had a major hand in the design of the UNM basketball arena, among other projects. After a stint with VISTA in 1967-68, he returned to Santa Fe and was variously occupied as a cabinet maker, employee of several architectural and engineering firms, a cab driver, Sunday school superintendent and a businessman.

In 1970-71, he formed his own loom company. His growing business put him in almost daily contact with people from all callings who were interested in weaving but could not afford the necessary loom. He investigated and discovered that a concise manual on loom building, using simple materials, had never been published. He decided to give it a whirl, and thus did Tim Reed become an author, as well.

To you all — may you develop your talents independently and preserve yourself and the fruits of your talents from Madison Avenue and other such imprisonments.

INTRODUCTION

This manual is designed for the absolute beginner in the world of purchasing wood and building a loom. The loom is designed in such a way that to build it you only drill the holes and install the screws, nuts and bolts. No cutting is required, and you need to plan for only about sixty hours construction time.

You can build this loom out of supplies to be found at any lumber store, using simple hand tools to be found in most average households. The one item which is too complicated to fabricate is the reed. This you will have to order, and you should do it as early in the game as possible. Write to Nilus Leclerc, L'Isletuille 6, Quebec, Canada, for a list of loom and parts distributors in your area. After selecting the distributor closest to you, place an order for a 40-inch reed. If you do not have an idea what you want for a dent count, get either a twelve or eight dent for starters.

The loom that will result from your efforts is a 40-inch, counterbalanced, four harness loom. The *40-inch* refers to the width of the woven material. *Counterbalanced* is a type of mechanism in the loom used to raise and lower the *harness.*

Construction of this loom requires a space of at least eight feet by eight feet, but ten feet by ten feet is better. Also, build the loom in the space or room you plan to use for weaving. The loom can be moved, but this requires disassembling, and even though this is simple, repeated disassembling would not be healthy for the loom.

In this manual, we will approach the loom from two major directions. They are: 1) what materials are used and how to get them, and 2) the process of making the parts and then assembling them. Actually, we will isolate the separate elements of the loom-building process into manageable units and examine them one by one before putting them all together.

As an added help, there is a glossary and three pages of standard construction drawings at the back of this manual. The glossary will help explain terms you may not at first understand. You may, and probably should, consult the standard construction drawings before, during and after your loom-building adventure. These drawings also would be of help to experienced woodworkers who might want to alter the standard plans to produce a fancier loom.

Now to tackle the loom. Your first line of attack is to read this manual through, first word to last, to familiarize yourself with what's happening. Doubtless, there will be things you won't understand right away, but don't despair because as the loom becomes a three dimensional reality under your hands, the answers to your questions will become self-evident. With that, on with the loom!

1. HOW TO SAY "BREAST BEAM" IN LUMBER LANGUAGE.

The first element of loom building we are going to examine is the materials involved. In fact, we are going to learn lumberyard language — the technical side, as we will be rubbing elbows with carpenters, cabinetmakers, lumbermen, mechanics and probably others.

There are two large classifications to consider — wood and fasteners, and we will start with wood. When we talk lumberyard talk about wood, we use words like *two by four, parting stop* and equally incomprehensible terms and phrases. In loom talk, we use *breast beam, lams* and the like. Do the two mix? Yes, they do. Here is how. The breast beam is made from a two by four (2" x 4") and the lams are made from screen stock, and so forth. So, let's begin to isolate the lumberyard talk we need to know.

The spoken phrase *two by four* is written as 2" x 4". These numbers are the approximate dimensions in inches of the cross section of a piece of lumber. If we say, 2" x 4" by 50-3/4", we have told the lumber man what we want in terms of thickness, width and length. However, we still haven't given him a complete picture. To get all the message across, we need to say, in this order, how many of what, in what length, and what grade of lumber we want. In lumberman's language it goes like this, *seven pieces of 2" x 4" by 50-3/4", number 2.* What we have said is we want seven pieces of two by four cut to measure fifty and three-quarters inches long and that we want two grade lumber.

The grade is important. The lumber industry has a grading system to describe the quality of the material available, and we need in some cases to specify the grade. Grading goes as follows: "select" means no knots and straight or not warped; *number two* (#2) means few knots and straight or not warped; *number three* (#3) means many knots and not straight. (We won't use number 3 for our loom.) Almost all material one inch thick or less is graded "select", and for two by four stock, number two grade is the best the lumber industry makes. So when we talk about two by four's in lumber, we only have to say how many pieces of 2" x 4" at what length of #2.

The same pattern applies to one by four (1" x 4") material. When written it looks like this, *eight pieces, 1" x 4" by 43-7/8", select.* We have said the same things as we did about 2" x 4"s except that the term 1" x 4" means we are talking about a plank approximately one inch thick and four inches wide.

Again, we have specified the length we want. Be sure to take note of the cut length. The construction industry generally doesn't order cut lengths of lumber from a yard. They take the lumber at the length it comes off the truck. In our case, we must ask for the cutting service. This service is usually offered at minimal or no charge, but we do have to ask for it. In the case of talking 1" x 4" lumber, when we say *1" x 4" x 43-7/8"*, we automatically have asked for the cutting service. The same is true for 2" x 4" by 50-3/4". So, when we specify length we are saying cut length of either select or #2 material.

Now that we know about talking 2" x 4" and 1" x 4", we will add to our knowledge by talking about 1" x 2". This term looks like the others so it ought to work in the same way. It doesn't. Why? Because the construction industry's demands have caused the lumber industry to supply only standard types of material, and their coding system reflects this. The 1" x 2" falls into a different category than 1" x 4" or 2" x 4" by use. What we will say to the lumberyard man about 1" x 2" is this; *Give me six pieces of 1" x 2" screen stock thirty-one inches long.*

We are using the same pattern as we did with the 2" x 4" and 1" x 4" in asking for a number of pieces at a certain length. However, we left out the grade which we had specified for 1" x 4" or 2" x 4" material. Actually, the grade is implied because 1" x 2" screen stock only comes in select grade since, believe it or not, it is used primarily for making screen doors. So we don't have to worry about the grade of 1" x 2" since there is only one. Remember, though, we must use the words *screen stock* to be sure the message is heard.

Now, we know about screen stock and 2" x 4"s and 1" x 4"s, so let's look at 1-3/8" stop, and stop we do. What on earth is 1-3/8" stop? Part of a telegram? No, it is just a different way of saying the same thing as 2" x 4" or 1" x 4". The term *stop* in lumber talk means the particular piece of wood that the door bangs against when you shut it. It is actually the *door stop.* If we say 1-3/8" stop we are talking about a piece of wood which is approximately 1/2" thick and 1-3/8" wide. There are different shapes of stop, and we want square. To get what we want, then, we say, *I need two pieces of square 1-3/8" stop, 1/2" thick and 48" long.* As with the screen stock, the grade is implied since there is only one — select.

Now it is time to reflect on what lumber talk we have learned so far. In lumber we say how many, of what, how long, and sometimes, in what grade. In the case of 1" x 4"s and 2" x 4"s, we say something like, *six pieces 2" x 4" by 50-3/4", #2.* For 1" x 2", we ask for *six pieces 1" x 2" screen stock, 31".* Remember, we don't have to specify grade for 1" x 2"s or stop since the grade is implied, and remember, too, we have asked for the cutting service when we specify the length of pieces we want. So, there it is — how many pieces of what (in terms of thickness and width), and how long, with the grade either specified or implied.

But, we are not through talking about the lumber we need yet. Our next adventure is learning about lattice. Rose and vine trellises and grape arbors are made of this stuff. Lattice is a piece of wood, like 2" x 4", of given thickness, which is approximately 1/4", but the width varies from 1-1/8" to 1-3/4". We will be using 1-1/8" lattice. You ask for lattice the same way you ask for all other lumber we have studied so far, and it goes like this: *eight pieces 1-1/8" lattice, 41 inches long.* Here again, the grade is implied (select) and we have requested that the length be cut.

The next to the last wood item is no problem. All we need to know how to say is *three-quarter inch and dowel.* We stick these words into the familiar pattern of how many, of what length and which grade, and we ask for *"two pieces three-quarter inch dowel".* Note there is no length called out in this request. The reason for this is that most lumber companies stock dowel in only thirty-six inch lengths, which is the exact length we need for the loom in two places. You will see later, when you start reading over the materials list, that you will request cut lengths of three-quarter inch dowel to make some parts for the loom. Those requests will go, *four pieces 3/4" dowel, 5-1/2 inches long, one piece 3/4" dowel, 4 inches long,* and *one piece 3/4" dowel, 1-1/2 inches long.* As with all the other wood items except 2" x 4" and 1" x 4", the grade is implied.

Fortunately, we are about through! We have only two more wood items we need to learn to describe in lumberyard talk. The first of these items is what the lumber industry calls a *full round.* This is not describing a person's physical characteristic; it is a term used to describe a large, round, rod-like stick which is made to the diameter of 1-1/8" or 1-3/4". In the construction industry these are used mostly as wood closet hanger rods. Since we are talking about a piece of wood that has a circular cross section, it obviously has only the diameter to be worried over and no width. In lumber we ask for one piece of 1-1/8" full round, forty inches long. The grade is implied and the cut length is requested.

The last wood item we need to know how to ask for is *parting stop*. This is the label given to the little strip of wood which is used to separate the moving window frames in double hung windows. The size available that we will use for the loom is 1/2" x 3/4". What we ask for is, *two pieces 1/2" x 3/4" parting stop, 41 inches long.* The grade is again implied.

Finally, we are through the woods. What have we learned? We have learned to talk in lumber talk about wood to lumberyard people. We first say how many, then we say of what, be it 2" x 4"s or 3/4" dowel. Next, we say to what length we want it cut. And, finally, we specify the grade for 2" x 4" and 1" x 4" material, remembering that the grade of other wood pieces for the loom is implied and there is no need to call it out.

2. HOW TO SAY "HINGE" IN LUMBER LANGUAGE.

The world of metals and metal fasteners is not as obviously organized as the world of lumber, if you can call a haystack organized. We still use the pattern of how many of what, but in most cases how long and what grade is not used. Let's take a look at what we will use, keeping in mind that some of the names given fasteners are self-explanatory, while others are obscure.

Now that you have taken a peek at the illustration of fasteners, you can see the eye bolt has an eye, the *U* bolt looks like a "U" and the wing nut has wings. Where is the lag on the lag screw and the carriage on the carriage bolt? This is only part of the obscurity in lumberyard language, and you will find that even most lumberyard people can't explain the terms.

However, for our purposes, we need only have a minimal visual awareness and verbal knowledge of each item. As in lumber, when placing an order for fasteners, we will have to know the language that the salesman understands. The standard pattern of how many of what applies. Sometimes we specify length; however, no grade is called out.

The first fastener in the illustration is an eye bolt. The critical information you need for the salesman is: *5/16" eye bolt with a 3/4" diameter hole and a length of three or four inches.* The design of the loom is such that either length eye bolt will do the job with ease, so if one length is not in stock, you can use the other.

If we look at the next item in the illustration on fasteners, we see a flat thing with a cylinder running the length of the middle. I am sure this isn't the first time you have seen a hinge, but if you want to refresh your memory, go look at the hinges on your door. Notice that they swing about a pin at the center.

What we will have to ask for are two types of hinges. One type is called a hinge, oddly enough, and the other is called a butt. The difference is that the pin is removable in the butt, and we need this; however, the pin in the hinge is fast (not removable). When you place your order, say, *I want one pair of three inch half surface iron butts and three pairs of one and one-half inch utility hinges.* The term *half surface* means that half of the hinge is designed to show and the other half is designed to be between the door and the frame, if you put it on a door and frame. We need this type — the half surface type — for our loom, so be sure to specify.

Following the hinge in the illustration, we find *lag screws.* Why they are called lag screws is one of those unanswered questions we will just have to live with. However, the thing to note about lag screws is the way they compare with other screws. All lag screws have a hexagonal head requiring a wrench to fasten. The heads on other screws have slots or holes. The information we need to relate to the man behind the counter about lag screws goes like this. *I need forty-four 1/4" x 2-1/2" lag screws.* In talking about lag screws, we first say how many, and we always refer to the diameter (1/4") before talking about the length (2-1/2").

The next item illustrated, as the shape indicates is an *S* hook. To get our message across, we request *six S hooks 1-1/4".* The 1-1/4" describes the largest dimension on the hook. If they don't have this size in stock, take the next size, either way. Note that we again say how many of what.

Getting screw eyes from a lumberyard man presents a number of obstacles which need to be taken into account. Most lumber companies just dump screw eyes into bins which are open to the public. Therefore, a lot of rooting is sometimes necessary to get what you need. But, anyway, we say, *I need seventy screw eyes about 1-3/8" long with a 1/4" eye.* This gets the message across. Since he may have to go to a lot of bother getting them, the salesman may ask what they are going to be used for. Here is your chance to spout off some loom talk. Tell him the eyes will be used for the tie-ups between the treadles and lams, and he will be in the dark, as you once were when lumber people talked lumber talk.

Then, you will need to ask for *one set of 3/8" x 2" flat corner irons,* shown in the illustration.

Next to the corner iron in the illustration are the wood screws. When dealing with wood screws, the pattern is describing the *what*. With the lag screws and carriage bolts, we called out the diameter first and then the length. Wood screws, wouldn't you know it, are just the opposite. We must, after saying how many (42), call out the length (1-1/2") followed by the diameter. The diameter is expressed by gauge and not inches, and is represented by a number like *4*. In addition, we have to describe the characteristics of the screw head. For this loom we need concern ourselves with only flat and round head screws. So, when placing the order we say something like, *I want forty-two, 1-1/2" No. 8 flat head wood screws.*

The next illustrated fastener we need is called a *U* bolt. Again, we need to say how many, in this case four. Then we need to describe what it is. We simply say we need *four 1/4" by 1-1/8" U bolts.* The 1-1/8" refers to the diameter around which the bolt rod is turned to form the U.

We are now at the point of learning about *carriage bolt*. The part which sets a carriage bolt apart is the head. The head has no slot or holes or any other handle to allow you to grab it from the head end. The way the bolt grips is by crushing the shoulders under the head into the wood surface, forming a box which then presses against the shoulders of the bolt. As you get into using these bolts, this process will become evident. To tell the lumberman we want this type of bolt, we use the same technique as with lag screws. We say we want eight 1/4" by 2-1/2" carriage bolts. The 1/4" refers to the diameter of the rod used to form the bolt, and the 2-1/2" refers to the length from the point where the shaft and head meet to the end of the threaded part.

Corner braces, next in the illustration, follow a similar pattern. We need four sets of 1-1/2" corner braces, and they come packaged two to a set, so we actually will be getting eight corner braces in all.

The wing nut illustration after the corner braces is probably the easiest to ask for. We simply say we need two 1/4" wing nuts. The 1/4" refers to the diameter of the hole through the nut. The wings are handy since they facilitate installation and removal without the use of a wrench. With the exception of these wing nuts, we need not order nuts as a separate item. Be sure, however, to check each and every bolt you order to see that it has a nut.

Although not the last to be discussed, the last item illustrated is the surface bolt. These are all over the place. You usually find them on French doors and double doors, and they act as a latch. To get what we need we say, *I want one 4" surface bolt.* If they don't have it in stock, have it ordered or go on to the next lumber store.

We already have discussed carriage bolts and seen them illustrated so we now need to talk about *machine bolts.* Imagine a simple bolt with no fancy stuff on it and you have imagined a machine bolt. We probably would get what we need if we were to simply ask for two 5/8″ by 4″ bolts. However, we will sound more knowledgeable and get what we really need by saying, *I want two 5/8″ by 4″ machine bolts.* Be sure to check and see if the nuts are on all the bolts when you get them on the counter.

Finally, we must ask for washers. A washer looks like a dime with a hole in it. They go onto the threaded part of a bolt sticking out of the wood before the nut is screwed on, and they are placed there to keep the nut from tearing up the wood as the nut is tightened. For our needs, we get 118, 1/4″ washers. The 1/4″ describes the diameter of the hole in the middle. We also will need to ask for *thirteen rivet burrs* which are simply small washers. If the salesman asks what size rivet burr, say, *1/8″.* Also request *one 3/8″ washer.*

Securing the nails you need will require a lot of explaining. The reason for this is that nails are sold by the pound or part thereof, and what we need doesn't amount to a pound. We want eightpenny common and sixpenny finishing nails. The term *penny* refers to the weight of the nail. *Common and finish* describe the nailhead characteristics. Ask for *two, eightpenny common nails and four, sixpenny finishing nails.* You want nails, not pounds of nails, but if you can't get the individual nails, ask for a quarter pound of each.

Rope is not such a problem. Ask for a roll of mason's line, preferably cotton, although nylon can be used. You also need 130 feet of 1/8″ nylon rope. Also in the category of rope is the carpet warp. It is a sure thing that your lumber store will not stock carpet warp, so you'll need to go to a yarn or macramé supplier for a spool.

This completes the section on fasteners and other types of hardware and materials. To get the message across about fasteners, we must say how many and then what. This is the pattern to which salesmen in lumberyards are oriented. In describing the *what* there are two major variations in fastener language. Bolts and lag screws are described first by diameter in inches and then length in inches. Wood screws are described first by length in inches and then diameter in gauge measure.

By now, you can consider yourself pretty adept at talking to lumberyard people. Take note, however, to go to a retail store since wholesale lumber outlets do not handle many fasteners nor do they cut to order.

In case you are by now worried about each and every piece of what you will be needing, here is the materials list.

MATERIALS LIST

Quantity	Description	Function on Loom
7	2″ x 4″ -50-3/4″ #2	Breast and back beams, lam frame, castle top
6	2″ x 4″-43″ #2	Horizontal side rails
4	2″ x 4″-30″ #2	Vertical upright at beams
2	2″ x 4″-47-1/2″ #2	Castle
2	2″ x 4″-25″ #2	Treadle frame
1	2″ x 4″-17″ #2	Lam leveler
8	1″ x 4″-43-7/8″ select	Cloth & warp beam
2	1″ x 4″-24″ select	Foot rest at sides of treadles
6	1″ x 2″ screen stock 31″	Treadles
4	1″ x 2″ screen stock 33″	Lams
2	1″ x 2″ screen stock 52-1/2″	Beater
2	1″ x 2″ screen stock 48″	Beater — horizontal mbrs.
4	1″ x 2″ screen stock 37-1/2″	Beater
2	1″ x 2″ screen stock 26-5/16″	Beater — vertical mbrs.
1	1″ x 2″ screen stock 26″	Warp beam ratchet release
2	1-3/8″ door stop 48″	Beater
1	1-3/8″ door stop 47″	Beater — horizontal mbrs.
8	1-1/8″ lattice 41″	Harnesses (heddle bar)
1	1-1/8″ full round 40″	Top roller
1	1-1/8″ full round 47-1/4″	Cloth beam
1	1-1/8″ full round 50″	Warp beam
2	3/4″ dowel full length of 36″	Harness rollers
4	3/4″ dowel 5-1/2″	Ratchet handle on cloth beam
1	3/4″ dowel 4″	Warp beam crank
1	3/4″ dowel 1-1/2″	Warp beam ratchet release
2	1/2″ x 3/4″ parting stop 41″	Apron bar
3 ea.	80-100-150 grit sand paper	
5	5/16″ eye bolt, 3/4″ diameter eye, 3″ or 4″	
1 pr.	3″ half surface iron butts	
3 pr.	1-1/2″ utility hinges	
44	1/4″ x 2-1/2″ lag screws	
8	1/2″ x 1″ lag screws	
6	S hooks 1-1/4″	
70	screw eyes, 1/4″ eye, 1-3/8″ long	
1	screw eye, 3/4″ eye	
1 set	3/8″ x 2″ flat corner irons	
24	3″ No. 12 flat head wood screws	
42	1-1/2″ No. 8 flat head wood screws	
20	1-1/4″ No. 4 flat head wood screws	
37	1″ No. 4 flat head wood screws	
7	3/4″ No. 4 round head wood screws	
4	1/4″ - 1-1/8″ U bolts	
8	1/4″ x 2-1/2″ carriage bolts	
2	1/4″ x 3″ carriage bolts	

1	1/4'' x 7'' carriage bolt
4 pr.	1-1/2'' corner braces
1	4'' surface bolt
2	1/4'' wing nuts
2	5/8'' x 4'' machine bolts
1	5/16'' nut
118	1/4'' washers
1	3/8'' washer
13	rivet burrs
2	eightpenny common nails
4	sixpenny finishing nails
1 roll	mason's line, preferably cotton
130 ft.	1/8'' nylon rope
1 spool	carpet warp (from macramé or carpet yarn shop)
1 roll	masking tape
1 pt.	stain
1	1'' brush
1 qt.	thinner
1 pt.	linseed oil or equivalent

3. WHERE TO GO AND WHAT TO DO WHEN YOU GET THERE.

As promised, I have just listed all the materials you will need to build your loom. The list is written so it closely resembles the sales slip the lumberyard will use. As you read through the list, you will find yourself recognizing all the things we discussed earlier.

After you feel you thoroughly understand the materials list, copy it down, rip it out, Xerox it, or take this entire manual with you to any retail lumberyard. The best time to go is in the middle of the week, when you are more likely to get the close attention you need.

Park your car in the yard parking lot around behind the store and go through what appears to be a back door. Corner the mildest looking salesman and sing out. He will start writing madly on his order form as you explain that these materials are for a loom and the wood pieces need to be cut as accurately as possible. If he resists, ask him then for as good a job as he or his personnel can do. The cuts can be off, but don't tell him.

After he has your order down, he may turn a pink or blue slip over to you and assume that you know everything since you so neatly described what you want. If this happens, don't panic; simply thank him and go back to the yard the way you came in. Upon arriving, you should be accosted by one of the yardmen. If you don't get fast service, however, open the trunk of your car. This usually panics the yard people and you will have a selection of helpers in short order.

They will then fill your order from the slip the salesman gave you. At this point you will again need to point out that the lengths of lumber must be cut as precisely as possible. Yard people usually hate being told what to do since the salesmen inside the air-conditioned, heated, clean, soft sales department are always sending out those impossible orders that have to be filled yesterday. Be kind. The yard people are at the bottom of the pecking order. They usually know what they are doing and have a good degree of skill, particularly if they have been around a while. However, some of these people tend to be careless and need to be watched. Just hanging around the saw while the lumber is being cut usually assures you of better performance.

Have all the cut wood parts and scraps put into your car and then return to the salesroom and corner your mild mannered salesman to fill out the fastener portion of your order. He may have done this already and will simply show you where your order is on the counter. If he starts talking about substitutions, listen carefully. Some substitutions can be tolerated; others cannot. The items which must be purchased exactly as specified are the butts, the U bolts, the corner irons, the carriage bolts, the corner braces, the wing nuts, the surface bolts, the machine bolts, the washers, the hinges and the lag screws. The wood screws can vary one gauge number larger, but avoid smaller gauges. The S hook can vary 1/4'' either smaller or larger.

After examining the substitutes and accepting them or rejecting them according to these few rules, make out an order for the fasteners not in stock, if there are some. The salesman has a form he will fill out which will ask for the identical information you gave him before. That is, how many of what. He will then tell you when he expects your order to be delivered. This could be a day or a week, so call him before coming in to pick up the rest of the order. (You may have to wait for some wood parts, too.)

After coming to some conclusion about the fasteners and/or the wood, hand back the order slip you took to the yard when you had the wood pieces cut. The reason for handing the slip back is that the salesman needs to see what wood parts were actually filled so he can charge accordingly. Yard people make a mark on the slip each time they have supplied individual items on an order slip.

At this point in the game, the salesman will ask if you want anything else. Depending on your response, he will go to the adding machine to add up the cost of your order. While he clacks away at the keys, you can nervously light a cigarette, if you are prone to smoking, and think of what wonderful times you had last summer instead of the dollars mounting up on his adding machine.

The bill, depending on your location, will be somewhere around $50. In smaller towns you can expect it to be slightly more; in large cities it will be less. When you look at the slip after it is all added up, you may be confused about what you are paying for, because next to the order for "7 pcs. 2" x 4" - 50-3/4" #2, you will see something like "3 pcs. 2" x 4" - 10' #2". Since the lumber milling company doesn't make special cuts for the construction industry or lumberyards, the yards will cut your pieces out of standard lengths and write them down as such even though the actual parts have been cut to length specified by you.

Your visit to the lumber company may vary a little from what I have just described, particularly if you live in a small town. So, if the system I just outlined is not used by your lumberyard, again just corner the mildest looking salesman and give him your order. He will start writing madly on his order form and then probably fill the order himself. All the requirements for precision cuts and the variations allowed for fasteners still apply. However, you have the advantage of explaining to only one person that you are building a loom. Getting good service will be fairly easy if you clearly say how many of what, etc., as outlined before.

To build your loom, you will need a few simple tools. Borrow them if you can. The tools needed are an eight inch or six inch adjustable wrench, a carpenter's square, a moderately priced tape measure and large and small screwdrivers. You also must have an electric drill and the following drill bits: 3/4", 5/8", 3/8", and 1/4" spade bits; and 3/16", 7/32", 9/64", 11/64", and 5/64" twist bits. Also get your hands on a countersink and an awl.

If you have never held a screwdriver or the like, go to your local library for the right books, or send for *How to Use Tools and Wood* at $1.25 from Pocket Books, division of Simon and Schuster Inc., 630 Fifth Ave., New York, N.Y., 10020. Don't buy a highly sophisticated cabinetmaker's text unless you have intentions of redesigning the loom with fancy joints and special woods.

4.   NOW I'VE GOT IT, WHAT DO I DO WITH IT?

Now that you have all the parts and pieces accumulated, you may find yourself asking, "I'm going to make a loom out of this pile of sticks? How can I ever make sense out of this mess?"

You can, simply by looking at the parts that are to make the whole and then by reconstructing these parts into the whole. We did this to learn lumber language, and we will do it again to learn the loom.

Let's begin by assuming that you know nothing about looms. I do not want to insult anyone's intelligence, but for the sake of many readers of this manual, I must include as much groundwork and information as possible to keep the project going.

Before getting into actual construction of your loom, you should develop an understanding of how a loom works. This may get dry, but keep a glass of your favorite refreshment handy and remember that understanding how a loom works will make building your loom much easier.

First, study Illustration 3 and don't be surprised if you find everything confusing. The diagram sort of looks like a loom, but doesn't look like one. That's because the supporting framework and harness moving mechanism have been left out. These will be explained in fuller detail later on. As you look at the diagram, keep in mind that the weaver sits or stands at the breast beam to do his weaving. The process of weaving is a simple one. For instance, you probably remember those extraordinarily long days in grade school when all you had to play with was your fingers. At some time or another you probably twisted them into each other, one finger over the other and under the next and so forth. That tangle of fingers was weaving. After you get your loom built, you will be tangling threads together in much the same way.

How does a loom do that? Take another look at the weaving schematic. You will see the harnesses illustrated. They spread the warp into sheds and then a filler is passed through. The next step in the process is to pass the filler through the shed and then press it into place with the beater. Then you raise the front harness and drop the back harness, giving you a shed opposite the one you began with. From there, you follow the same procedure as you followed before, and so on and so on. That is the principle, highly simplified.

I do not pretend to teach weaving. That is best left up to those who have published texts, and I strongly advise you ask at your local library or bookstore for basic weaving books, or send for "Step by Step Weaving" by Nell Znamierowski from Golden Press, Western Pub. Co., 850 Third Ave., New York, N.Y., 10022. This is an excellent manual and costs only $2.50.

5. I CAN'T BELIEVE I BUILT THE WHOLE FRAME.

Now that you have familiarized yourself with the loom schematics and feel you understand them, it is time to move into actual construction of your loom. Some of the language you have learned to recognize will appear as we go along, but if some of the words confuse you, remember you can look them up in the glossary at the back of this manual.

The framework for your loom is basically a box. Let's look at Illustration 4 which shows the completed framework without the counterbalance system, cloth and warp beams, harness, treadle and beater. How does the framework come from that pile of lumber you brought home from the lumberyard?

Remember ordering pieces of 2" x 4" x 50-3/4" #2 pine? Those pieces are to be the breast and back beams as well as the feet and castle top beam. They also are the lam frame beams. All these parts are shown in Illustration 4. So, rummage through the lumber pile and set these seven 2" x 4"s near the floor area in which you plan to build your loom. Next, dig out the castle frame pieces which are the 47-1/2" long 2" x 4"s. There are two. Also, find the four 30" 2" x 4"s and the six 2" x 4" x 43" pieces. Set these aside with the other pieces you have picked out.

Now, before screwing all the 2" x 4"s together we must drill some holes. Study Illustrations 4 and 5 before you begin, and note that the hands in Illustration 5 show the method of measuring and marking for holes using your tape measure and carpenter's square. Next, pull out four of the 2" x 4" x 43" pieces you have collected and set two of them aside. The first set of holes will be drilled in the top rail as indicated in Illustration 4. Drill the rail as shown and insert U bolts. Thread the nuts on the bolts, but tighten the nuts only to the point that the bolt shows at the face of the nut. Then, drill the bottom rail as indicated in Illustration 6. The hole you have just made is for the beater pivot which comes along much later.

Fasten the 47-1/2" beam to the bottom rail as illustrated, and be sure the pivot hole is near the bottom. Proceed to secure the rest of the 2" x 4" x 43" rails making sure that each is square. Remember to take special care to locate the top rail so the U bolt is fourteen inches from the front end.

The contraption you have just finished looks like an inverted telephone pole. Actually, it is the right side panel of your loom. The left side panel is made to the same dimensions and in the same order. But, since it is the side opposite the right side, it has to *pancake*. That is, if you were to put the two sides together, the horizontal 2" x 4"s would touch each other and the castle frames would be on the outside. One side is the mirror image of the other. If this is not clear, look through the illustrations some more until you're sure.

Build the left panel, remembering that the hole in the bottom rail goes toward the bottom. As with all the lag screw joints, use two screws with washer per joint. Having assembled the two trees, go on to attach the upright 2" x 4" x 30" pieces as shown in Illustration 4. Be sure the joints are square with the tree base, checking the squareness as demonstrated in Illustration 6. Drill with 3/16" bit and use two lag screws with washers per joint.

The next step is more complicated. Study the figure in Illustration 7 which shows the completed panels and the lam frame in three-quarter view. Also look at the detail of the left corner of the lam frame. Notice the repeated dimension of 47-1/2" and where this dimension falls on the frame. This dimension must be strictly adhered to.

The way to assemble the side panels is to set them upright — they should stand by themselves. Then, lay the lam frame (two of the 2" x 4" x 50-3/4" pieces) onto the middle 2" x 4" rail and move the frames out to the 47-1/2" required. The lam frames should stick out past the castle frame about 1/16" to 1/8".

Fasten one frame to one side with two lag screws and washers. At this point, you should check the trueness or squareness of that frame, as shown in Illustration 7. Next, go to the opposite side panel and adjust to 47-1/2", if necessary, and then fasten the two lag screws and washers. Check and adjust squareness and proceed the same way with the remaining frame member. If you have 8" clamps, you may use them here; however, they are not absolutely necessary.

The next step is to attach the castle top and the breast and back beams. If you have forgotten where they go, consult Illustration 6 again. Line up the castle top with the frame. Note that there is an overhang at both ends, similar to the overhang on the lam frames. This is natural, so don't panic. Drill and fasten one end of the castle top with one No. 12 screw. Then go to the other side and fasten it down with two No. 12 screws. (If the term No. 12 leaves you blank, they are the fattest of the three sizes of screws you have.) Finish securing the castle top by going back to the side you started first and put a screw into the corner hole you left vacant. Now, move on to the back beam and follow the same procedure as you followed with the castle top.

To attach the breast beam, first study the detail in Illustration 8 and then line up the breast beam as you did the castle top, making sure that there is an equal amount of overhang at each end. Next, get two strips of tape, preferably masking, about six inches long. These will hold the half-surface butts on the breast beam while you drive the screws. Place the tape on the short wing of the open butt. (This is not an X-rated term — it means hinge, remember?) The tape should be on the side where the screw heads will show. Position the butt to form a ninety degree angle with the pin on the outside and slip the butt between the breast beam and the upright supporting it. The tape should have its sticky side up and the pin should be on the outside.

Do the same on the other side of the beam. Center the butt and then wrap the tape around the breast beam on both ends. This is to hold the butt in place while removing the breast beam. Remove the beam and fasten the hinge onto it with the flat head screws provided in the butt kit. Next, turn the beam over and fasten the remaining butt leaves on the outside of the supporting uprights with the domed head screws that remain in the butt box. When this is done, the breast beam will be securely fastened to the supports, but it will be easy to remove when dressing the loom. As a trial, loosen and pry out the pins in the butts with a screwdriver and then replace them.

With the top, breast and back beams secure, turn the loom upside down so it rests on the castle top. The loom is upside down so you can put the feet on. They are the last 2" x 4" x 50-3/4" pieces left in your lumber pile. Either lean the loom frame against a wall to keep it upright, or put tape on the bottom rail and the feet to hold them in position while you are drilling and driving screws. But, be sure to securely support the frame while driving screws. Use chairs or books or whatever else is handy.

Follow the same procedure in driving the screws as you did for the castle top. That is, start at the corner of the foot and move around checking squareness as you go. Use No. 12 screws, two per joint. When the feet are secure, turn the whole business right side up and you should have a frame that looks like the loom frame in Illustration 7.

The next step is to drill 1/4" holes as indicated in the lam frame diagram in Illustration 8.

Now, you are ready to go on to the lams and treadles, but first, you might be ready for a short break from carpentry. It is, in other words, advisable at this point to apply the stain or other finish you desire, or you will find yourself leaving finger prints here and there on the bare wood. Before you begin the finishing, position the frame approximately where you expect to weave, and be sure to have newspapers around and under the loom.

The color of stain you select is a personal matter; however, it is advisable to stay away from dark stains. Dark stains are used to make light woods look like expensive, exotic dark woods, but even an untrained eye can pick out the fraud. If the extraordinary range of stain selections stumps you, use the fruitwood put out by the Minwax people. You will need one pint for the framework, and be sure to read and follow the directions on the can. You should allow the stain to dry at least 12 hours before beginning work on the rest of your loom.

Remember too that a loom is not designed to be an immaculate piece of furniture, so don't spend hours sanding, staining and waxing. On the other hand, you will find that staining the loom, although a simple matter, changes its character from every day cold 2" x 4"s into an intimate experience of wood grains and subtle changes in hue. And, when you finish it, you have made it your own.

6.   THE COUNTERBALANCE SYSTEM.

This section deals with the harness counterbalance system, the system that raises and lowers the weaving in process. As you can see from Illustrations 9 and 10, there are several parts to this system and, by nature of their tie-up, they are all interdependent. To make things simpler, we will separate the mechanism into four major elements. They are the lams, harnesses, rollers and treadles. You can pick out some of these by studying the two illustrations.

To begin construction, pull out the following pieces from your pile of lumber: the six pieces of screen stock measuring thirty-one inches — these will become the treadles; four pieces of screen stock measuring thirty-three inches — these are the lams; the eight pieces of 1-1/8"-41" lattice — to become the heddle bars in the harness; the 1-1/8" full round measuring forty inches — to be used as the top roller; and the two 3/4" x 36" dowels — to be used as harness rollers.

Now that you have all these wood pieces separated, don't chop them into kindling in despair. Rather, go to your loom frame and pull the hinge pins out of the butts so you can remove the breast beam. You will be constantly moving in and out of the frame and the breast beam just gets in the way.

Lam Making —

Now that everything is set, you can progress. Find the lams. Lay them flat and drill a 1/4" hole 1-1/8" from the left end of each one as shown in the lam section of Illustration 11. Next, drill a 5/64" hole twenty-three inches from the left end on the top of each lam. Don't drill too deep since these and the following holes are for the screw eyes and you need to leave enough wood to hold the screws securely. When you have completed this, turn the lam over and drill six 5/64" holes in the bottom of each lam. The first hole is to be 14-7/8" from the left end as illustrated, and the rest are 3-1/4" apart.

Then, lucky person, you get to screw 52 screw eyes into all of those little holes. Use your wrench or stick your awl through the eyes to give you leverage, making the job easier. The final positioning of the eyes should be such that you can sight through them down the top and bottom of the lam.

When the excitement of twisting all those little eyes in has died down, you can install the lams with the 1/4" x 7" carriage bolt. To do this, grab all the lams and take them, the bolt and a handful of washers to the loom frame. The lams go in the space between the 2" x 4" lam frames that you put in the middle of the frame some time ago. If you need to refresh your memory, take a look at Illustration 7 again and locate the lam frame there. Then, stick the carriage bolt into the 1/4" hole on the left end of the front cross member of the lam frame. Slip a washer on the bolt when it comes through and then mount a lam on the bolt, making sure when you do that the top is the top. You will know because the top of the lam has only one screw eye. Slip a pencil under the right end of the lam on top of the frame to hold the lam in place. Stuff the bolt through and when it appears at the far side of the lam, slip on another washer. Keep mounting lams and stuffing washers until there are no more lams.

At this point there will be a little space between the fourth lam and the rear cross member. You are now faced with the problem of slipping enough washers on to fill the gap, but once again modern technology comes to the rescue. Remember how you used tape to temporarily fasten the butts on the breast beam? You can use the same type of tape to solve the present problem. Take a washer and stick it on the end of a piece of tape and drop it into the slot and slip it onto the bolt. Following the same process, test with another washer to see if there is enough room for it. When the lams are snug but not stiff on the carriage bolt, put the nut on and tighten it. Your finished effort should have all the tops to the top, showing only one screw eye per lam. The lams should be happily resting on a pencil or equivalent at the right and pivoted on a carriage bolt at the left.

Roller Fabrication —

The next portion to deal with is the roller system. The wood pieces you will use are the 1-1/8" x 40" full round, the 3/4" x 36" dowels, the 3/4" No. 4 round head screws, rivet burrs, and the S hooks. You will also use some of the 1/8" nylon rope.

Begin assembly by marking off the centers of the full rounds and the dowels as demonstrated in Illustration 12. In order to find the center of the 3/4" dowel, you will need to draw what looks like a square and then draw an X by connecting the corners. Accuracy is very, very important. If you mark the holes off center and subsequently fasten the screws that way, your system will work clumsily.

Drill the screw holes in the ends of all the full rounds and dowels with a 5/64" bit. Slip two rivet burrs on the No. 4 round head screw and drive them into the end. Leave enough room between the screw heads and the dowel and full round ends to allow the rivet burrs and S hooks to turn freely, as indicated in Illustration 12.

Then, go to the loom frame and prepare to measure on the under face of the castle top beam. Start from the left side at the corner and first measure off and mark a point 3-3/8" from the corner in the center of the underside. Then, again from the left underside corner, mark off a point 43-9/16" in. Drill through these points with a 1/4" bit. These are the holes through which you will feed the rope that supports the full round.

Once the holes are drilled, you are ready for the rope. Cut two pieces of 1/8" nylon cord three feet long. Push the middle of this length through the holes you just drilled and hang the S hooks on the loop. Temporarily tie these ropes by wrapping them around the castle top and knotting the ends together. Be sure the S hooks are relatively level. Slip the full round on the S hooks by placing the hooks between the rivet burrs.

Then cut two pieces of 1/8" nylon cord twenty inches long. Knot the ends around the S hooks with a figure eight knot as demonstrated in Illustration 13. Fiddle around adjusting the knots until there is exactly sixteen inches between each knot. Now, run these cords three times around the full round at each end. Position the S hooks so they are relatively level and slip the 3/4" dowel into the hooks the same way you placed them on the full round.

By this time, you probably have discovered that if you slip one dowel in on one side, it will pull the cord and fall. The solution to this is to mount both dowels at one end at the same time and then mount the other ends. To level these dowels and locate the final position for the hanger cords, push up on the cord at a point just under the full round. Don't try to level by pulling on the cord, since this just tightens it and you get nowhere.

Next, cut four lengths of 1/8" nylon cord eighteen inches long and tie figure eight knots in the ends. Again, you will need to fiddle around with the knots until you have exactly twelve inches between them as you see in Illustration 13. These knots will serve as the *buttons* for the harness. Run these newly knotted lengths around the dowels three times about two inches from the ends. Then, just let them dangle there and note your progress.

You have all these rollers and hanger cords installed, and that's something you probably will want to marvel at for a while!

After playing with the rollers, use some leftover string or twine to tie a loop around the whole assembly including the castle top. This will keep the rollers from going up and down while you are installing the harness which happens to be the next step.

Harness Construction —

For the harness, first gather up the eight pieces of forty-one inch lattice you piled up a while back and lay them flat for drilling. They are to become the top and bottom heddle bars as shown in Illustration 11. Now, make a mark nine inches from each end of four of the lattice pieces. Proceed to mark off another point 1/2" in from one side at the nine inch mark and drill these points with a 7/32" bit. These four pieces make up the bottom heddle bars, and the 7/32" holes will be tied to the lams.

On the bottom heddle bars just drilled, drill another hole, this one to receive the heddle bar brace, as illustrated. The hole, to be drilled with a 7/64" bit, needs to be at the top outside corner, roughly one-half inch in from both the top and the outside edges. You drill these holes at both ends of the bottom heddle bars so that when you're finished you will have drilled eight holes nine inches in from the ends and eight holes near the upper corners as shown in both Illustrations 11 and 14.

Now you are ready to drill the top heddle bars, the four remaining pieces of forty-one inch lattice. With the 7/64" bit still in the drill, drill the holes as shown in Illustration 11. These holes are located one-half inch in from both the ends and the bottom edges of the bars.

The next step is to tie the buttonholes on the top heddle bars. If you have done macramé, you will probably recognize the good old square knot. Cut eight twelve inch lengths of mason's line and if it is nylon, heat the ends to prevent fraying. Follow Illustration 14 for tying the buttonholes. Position each buttonhole about four inches in from the ends of the bars. Note from the illustration that the buttonholes are to stick up only one inch about the bar. This will take some adjusting and readjusting to accomplish, and you probably will get frustrated in the process. But, surviving the making of the eight holes calls for a celebration, so hang the bars on the buttons. When you do this, the need for the loop will become obvious. Again hang two ends at a time and start with the back set of bars. It is a lot of fun playing with the set up at this point, so enjoy, enjoy! And, while you're at it, you can move the hangers so they are all hanging straight.

Heddles for the Harness —

Start the heddle process by cutting lengths of carpet warp or equivalent to lengths of approximately thirty inches. You will need at least 640 of same, but don't despair of spending a week at it, since there is an easy way. That easy way is to wrap the heddle material around the exposed uprights which normally support the breast beam. Make a total of 210 passes, grouping the warp at about a hundred passes per group. Then, tie two keepers around the strands at the center. Cut the strands between the keepers, releasing the carpet warp from the uprights. You will then have a number of eight-foot pieces which you next cut into thirds, giving you approximately 300 strands of carpet warp thirty inches long, plus or minus. Repeat the process when you need more strands.

To make the heddle board, grab a piece of scrap lumber from somewhere and gather up four, sixpenny finishing nails. Drive the points of two of these nails into the scrap lumber eleven inches apart and draw a straight line between them. On that line mark a point 5-1/4" from each nail. This should leave a gap of one-half inch between the points. Drive the two remaining nails one-half inch into the lumber at the 5-1/4" points marked earlier. Then, mark one end of the lumber with a smile or the letters T O P; this will immediately tell you where the top is.

Place this heddle making board on your lap with the top away from you as you tie the carpet warp into heddles in stacks of ten with the tails at the bottom. Tying the heddles is demonstrated in the section of Illustration 14 dealing with the heddle board. As you can see, you will have a square knot below the last three nails on the board. The little one-half inch section of the heddle between the two middle nails is called the *eye*. Avoid tying granny knots, since they are unstable as any good scout will tell you.

When you have a stack of ten tied, clip the tails and distribute your heddles along the top heddle bars. Each harness takes 160 heddles. Slip in the bottom heddle bars during the process of distributing the heddles along the bar. If you are confused about how these little pieces of carpet warp should look when they are on the heddle bars, turn back to Illustration 9 and take a look. You will see the top heddle bars in place, the eyes loose in the center and the bottom heddle bars in place.

When all the heddles are finished and distributed, cut eight pieces of mason's line twenty-eight inches long. Feed these through the holes you drilled in the corners of the top heddle bars. These should be one piece of line per hole. Then, feed one end of each line through the corner hole in the bottom bar and draw the line through the corner hole in the bottom bar and draw the line just tight enough to slacken the heddles to the point that the eyes can be pulled one-quarter inch off dead center without pulling up the bottom bar. Tie the mason's line with the ever present square knot as shown in Illustration 14.

With all the heddles in place, you are at the point of tying the harness to the lams. First, cut four lengths of one-eighth inch cord 3-1/2" feet long. Thread one end of each of these cords through the screw eyes on the lam tops. (Remember? You put those screw eyes in some time ago!) Start with the back heddle bar and expose the left hole in that bar by separating forty heddles to the left. Push the remaining heddles to the right, leaving a space about one-half inch between the two groups.

Then, tie the left end of the 3-1/2 foot cord to the heddle bar with a half hitch as demonstrated in the heddle bar section of Illustration 14. Do this on the left side of all four bars. Next, go to the right side of the harness and separate forty heddles to the right of each hole as was done with the left side and tie each lam to its harness with a temporary knot. Again, check Illustration 9 if you want to refresh your recollection about how all this should look when it's in place.

At this point, you can remove that pencil or equivalent that has been supporting the lams all this time. Let the lams sink while you run to your lumber pile for the 2" x 4" x 17" wood piece. Check to see how this piece fits between the two cross members of the lam frame. If it is not a loose fit, sand or scrape it with a knife until it is loose. Then, drive the two, eightpenny nails one inch from one end on each side. These are to act as pivots. Place the 2" x 4" in the space at the right side. Now, fuss with the temporary knots of the draw cords until all the harnesses are level.

Treadle Creation —

The last operation in this series is assembling the treadles and the treadle carriage. We will start with the latter by collecting the two 2" x 4" x 25" and the two 1" x 4" stock twenty-four inches long.

Lay the 2" x 4"s parallel to each other and flat for drilling. The 1" x 4"s are then placed on top of the 2" x 4"s, also parallel, so that a square is shaped with the 2" x 4"s on the bottom. You can see a real life drawing of the treadle carriage in Illustration 9.

Screw the 1" x 4" stock to the 2" x 4"s with two 1-1/2" No. 8 flat head screws per joint. Keep the frame square by drilling and driving only one screw at first. Then adjust the 1" x 4" stock until it is square with the 2" x 4". You can then drill a second hole and drive the screw. Go to the other end of the 2" x 4" and repeat the operation. Attach the remaining 2" x 4" squaring it with only one side, since the other side will take care of itself.

Put this assembly in its approximate location in the loom, below the breast beam on the floor.

To build the treadles, collect the thirty-one inch screen stock. There should be six pieces. Mark a guide line for the utility hinges one-half inch from one end of the stock, perpendicular to the sides. You should use the carpenter's square in this operation, since the hinge pins must be square with the length of the treadle, and the ends of the stock are not cut accurately enough to use as a square edge.

Next, attach the hinges with the edge of one leaf against the guide line and center the hinge in the width of the stock. Use the 5/64″ drill bit for the screw holes after marking their center with an awl. If you want to take a look at Illustration 11 you can see what the fully mounted treadle looks like and get a visual idea of what you need to do.

After attaching six hinges, flip all the treadles face up with the hinges down. Mark four points seven-eighths inches from the end opposite the hinge on each treadle. The points should be on the center line of the treadle and should run lengthwise. Punch with an awl to mark and then drill these points with a 5/64″ drill bit. Then, lucky you, screw in twenty-four screw eyes just to the point that they start to punch out at the back. When the screwing gets tight, use your adjustable wrench. The eyes should be positioned so you can sight through them down the length of the treadle.

With this done, you are ready to mount the treadles on the carriage. Make a mark on the carriage at the center of the space between the 1″ x 4″'s on the outside 2″ x 4″. That outside 2″ x 4″ is the one closest to you as you face the loom. Measure from that center mark 1-5/8″ to both sides and then draw parallel lines across the 2″ x 4″ where you have marked it. These lines establish the center of the hinge. Continue from these first two lines marking parallel lines 3-1/4″ apart.

When that is finished, turn the treadles so the screw eyes face the floor pointing away from the loom. Locate the center of the free hinge leaf and mark that center with a pencil. Place the edge of the loose leaf on the 2″ x 4″ and line the center mark up with the line you marked before on the 2″ x 4″. Position the loose leaf so the hinge pin is just at the edge of the 2″ x 4″ and then poke a hole in the center of one of the leaf's screw holes. Do not drill. Drive only one screw. When that screw is secure, flip the treadle over so it rests on the carriage. Then, line the treadle up so it is parallel with the frame, taking care to compensate for the sway caused by the looseness of the hinge. When it is parallel, carefully lift the treadle back over and install the remaining screw. Continue in the same manner for the remaining five treadles. Be sure each treadle is parallel with the sides of the treadle carriage.

When all treadles are in place, you are ready to attach the carriage frame to the loom. Begin by slipping the twenty-six inch length of screen stock on edge between the treadle carriage's outside 2″ x 4″ and the loom foot. Then measure 23-3/8″ from the left upright to the center of the space between the middle of the treadles. Fasten the treadle frame to the loom foot at this center point with two 1-1/2″ No. 8 flat head wood screws. Then, remove the twenty-six inch screen stock and you are done.

Positioning Harnesses in Loom —

Setting the heddle eye level is a precise operation. First, retie those safety loops we talked about earlier so there is enough room to allow the roller apparatus to drop about two inches. Tie these safety loops securely because chasing the rollers and heddles across the floor and then trying to get them all straightened out again isn't much fun. Next, cut pieces of string 4-1/2 to 5 feet long and tie them in clusters of four to the back beam, one cluster at the right side, the other at the left.

These strings should be positioned on the back beam so they can be drawn straight through the center of the four heddle eyes on each end of the harness apparatus. Now, draw the strings through the heddle eyes and be sure that one string goes through only one eye in only one heddle and that all four heddles have strings running through their heddle eyes.

Replace the breast beam you took off when you started this harness business and wrap the ends of the string tight around the breast beam. This will give you an approximation of the heddle eye level. Loosen the supporting cord you tied earlier to hold the top roller and ease the harness apparatus down to the point at which the strings running through the heddle eyes are straight and taut. Retie the top roller cord. Do the same at the other end of the loom with the four remaining strings and when you're finished, the heddle eyes should be level.

These various tie-ups will stretch out for a while and repositioning will be necessary occasionally. Don't panic. Just follow the same process you've just gone through to relevel the heddle eyes. The stretching will stop after you've used the loom a while.

Now, remove the safety loops and tie the lams to any four treadles individually. The method of tying lams to the treadles is sketched out in Illustration 11. You see that you use two fourteen inch lengths of mason's line per tie-up for this purpose. Make any final adjustments of lams or eye levels necessary and then remove strings and the breast beam. Playing around with the set-up as it now exists will give you some idea of the final experience of weaving on your own handmade loom.

7. BUILDING BEAMS.

After going through all that tying, you now untie the treadles so you can venture into building the cloth and warp beams. This is a complicated process, so before you begin any actual work with lumber and fasteners, reread this entire section to refresh your memory.

Then, pull out the eight 1'' x 4'' - 43-7/8'' pieces and the remaining two full rounds measuring 47-1/2'' and 50''. You will be drilling screw holes in the 1'' x 4's, so place them flat. Then, mark for holes 1-7/16'' from one edge both three inches and sixteen inches from each end. That makes four holes per piece for a total of thirty-two holes. See Illustration 15 for a picture of what the boards should look like when drilled.

Next, assemble four *T* shapes by laying on board on the two full rounds so the edge of the board coincides with the screw holes in an upright board which you now position. To check your work before screwing, stand at the right end of the T shape with the T leg facing you. Form a T with your hands using your right as the top of the T and your left as the leg. Roll the T to the right until your fingers point up on the right. This form should match the form of the 1'' x 4's as demonstrated in Illustration 15. Remember, the holes in the right 1'' x 4'' need to line up with the *leg* on the left 1'' x 4''. Note that the 1-7/16'' dimension on the left in Illustration 15 is the *top*. Use 1-1/2'', No. 8 flat head screw to secure the 1'' x 4's and then follow the same procedures and requirements to complete the remaining T's.

Now, assemble the T's into a swastika-like form around the full rounds using 1-1/2'' No. 8 flat head wood screws. Have 1-1/2'' of the full round stick out at the left end of each beam and keep the right end of the assembly as true as the wood will allow since this end is the ratchet end for the beams.

Next, grab the cloth beam which you can easily identify because it is the one with the shorter full round. Fasten the 1-1/2'' corner braces on the right end only of the cloth beam. Position the braces as shown in the cloth beam section of Illustration 16. Use a 5/64'' drill for the screw holes and fasten the screws in the little package the corner braces came in.

When the braces are in place, prepare to drill the eye bolt holes with a 3/8'' bit. These holes are to be three-fourths inches in from the right side and 1-1/4'' in from the outside edge as indicated in Illustration 16. Following this, mark a point on the short wing of the 1'' x 4's, one-half inch down from the edge and three-quarters inches in from the right side. Punch this mark with an awl but don't drill. Do this on all four sides of the cloth beam.

At this point, I must stick in some conceptual information. For some of you who have worked with looms before, this new concept will turn you wrong side out, since it reverses the ratchet system on the loom. Don't let this trip you up. Clear your mind of all those old ratchet systems and approach this new one calmly — it works, too!

All looms have some type of ratchet and/or brake system designed to hold the warp in tension while you are weaving. Historically, the ratchet gear has been fastened to the cloth and warp beams, and the dogs or prawls have been fastened to the frame, as you can see by looking at the drawing in the upper left corner of Illustration 17.

But, since we are dealing with supplies that are immediately available from your local lumber company, I have elected to redesign the ratchet mechanism to adapt to what is readily available. The design is unusual, yet it is very satisfactory and works happily. In the new design, we have moved the ratchet from the cloth beam and put it on the frame. The prawls then had to be moved so they fasten on the beam.

We didn't have to make many adjustments in the ratchet system for the warp beam, however, so that is fairly conventional.

With this explanation, we will begin work on the ratchet system. By looking closely at Illustration 17, you will see that the "ratchet teeth" are on the frame for the cloth beam and on the beam end for the warp beam. The hole location diagram in this illustration shows the positioning of the teeth. When you are ready to begin, tear out that page or trace the hole locations on a piece of paper and then transfer the diagram to the frame. Be sure to match the three-quarter inch hole you have already drilled to the hole represented in the diagram.

You should use a 7/64" drill bit to drill the holes for the 1/4" — 1" lag screws. You will find that the screw heads are positioned too close to one another to allow washers on each one, so use washers on alternate screws.

After drilling and installing all eight 1/4" — 1" lag screws, remove the U bolt from the left side frame member so you can install the beam. It is possible to get the cloth beam in backwards. To avoid this, study the drawing in Illustration 17. Note in the drawing that when the beam is resting with one 1" x 4" flat on top, its T leg points down and the vertical 1" x 4" is on the opposite side from the breast beam. This is the way your beam should look as you install it.

After inserting one end of the beam and assuring yourself that you have done it right, reinstall the U bolt. You will have to tighten the nuts by pressing one of the flats on the left side of the nut with a screwdriver and then tapping the end of the screwdriver with a hammer to rotate the nut. This is considered an immoral practice by cabinetmakers and other tool users. I consider it immoral, too, but it will just have to be done in this case. There is no need to have the nuts right. A snug fit will do the job. Stain the beams at this point.

Now that the cloth beam is installed and stained, the fun begins. Slip five washers on each eye bolt and insert it in the 3/8" hole you drilled in the cloth beam earlier. Thread on each nut and tighten. This whole process is outlined in the cloth beam section of Illustration 16. Do this for all sides of the cloth beam.

Now, fish out the remaining 1-1/2" corner braces and find the four 3/4" — 5-1/2" dowels. Pair off one corner brace and dowel. Lay the corner brace across one end of the dowel and then mark the centers of the corner brace holes which run along the length of the dowel. Punch the center point of each hole and drill two 7/64" screw holes in the side of the dowel as shown in Illustration 16. To hold the dowel while drilling, lay it in the slot between the first treadle and the frame. Keep the paired dowels and corner braces together as originally marked and drilled since not all corner braces have holes punched at exactly the same locations.

Remember when you were drilling holes to assemble the cloth beam? You punched a small hole on one end with an awl. Well, locate that punch mark now and place one corner brace on the beam with its inner hole centered on the punched mark three-quarters inches from the edge. If you do this right, the end of the brace will fit between two lag screw heads. Without drilling, drive a screw. This screw forms the end pivot on which the brace swings around, so do not drive the screw tight.

Now slip the dowel that was paired with the corner brace through the eye bolt. The leg of the corner brace which is to be screwed to this dowel should just touch the side of the dowel where you drilled the holes. If the two do not touch, reposition the brace by adjusting the pivot screw. Proceed in this manner for all the dowel brace pairs.

After completing this assembly, the function of the mechanism is fairly self-evident. To rotate the beam, grasp the closest dowel handle and turn the beam by pulling from the bottom of the beam towards yourself. This is the direction in which the cloth is advanced onto the beam. Twist the dowel handle to throw the corner brace leg into the space between two screw heads. By doing this you will see that the operation is similar to dropping a prawl into the teeth of a ratchet.

The ratchet mechanism on the warp beam is not quite so complicated. The ratchet teeth are formed with eight No. 12 screws and the two 3/8″ - 2″ flat corner irons. To begin the process, lean the warp beam against the loom frame with the long portion of the full round up. As you look down on the end, you should see the swastika-like shape swirling counterclockwise.

First carefully ream out the holes in the corner irons with a 7/32″ drill bit. Use a scrap piece of lumber to back up your work and drive a nail into the wood to slip the iron over to hold it while you are drilling. Now, lay the drilled out irons on the end of the beam. Leave a healthy 1/16″ between the edges of the irons and the outer edge of the 1″ x 4″s. Note that one hole in the iron is very close to the joint between the T leg and top. Don't be concerned. As long as some wood surrounds the screw it will work. The irons will distribute the load from that screw to the rest of the screws so there won't be too much stress on any single screw.

When you are ready to mount the corner irons, punch and drill the holes in the 1″ x 4″s with a 9/64″ bit. Drive the screws through the irons to the point that the heads are 5/16″ from the surface of the wood. Having driven the eight screws through the two corner irons, install the warp beam in the same fashion as you did the cloth beam.

As outlined in Illustration 16, mount the surface bolt on the frame at the center of the two U bolts holes. Be sure to use 1″ No. 4 flat head wood screws and not the ones supplied with the surface bolt because the screws supplied are too small and will not withstand the strain the bolt will take in operation. Slip the bolt into the guides and mount the guides one at the top of the frame, the other just above the U bolt holes. Drive the screws without drilling unless they are too difficult to turn.

Now find the twenty-six inch piece of screen stock which will become the ratchet release lever. Drill a hole in one sawed off end of this piece with a 7/32″ drill bit. Press the 1-1/2″ dowel half way through the big screw eye, the three-quarter inch eye, and turn the screw eye into the hole you have just drilled in the screen stock. This makes the handle facing the weaver. Rest the screen stock on the top of the 2″ x 4″ supporting the warp beam. Position it so the wide face of the stock touches the surface bolt and the stock's end is at the end of the 2″ x 4″ as shown in Illustration 15. This is the final position for this lever. Mark the stock at both sides of the bolt and then remove both the bolt and the lever.

You next will have to face the *strikes.* Find the package that held the surface bolt and read the instructions on the back of that package to find out what a *strike* is. Now, find the curved strike. Attach it to the bottom of the lever with the hole sticking out so the bolt can be slipped through it and be located at the two marks you just made. Do not drill the holes, just punch them. Then, slip the bolt through the curved strike hole so the knob will keep the bolt from falling out.

Now find the angle strike and *capture* the knob end of the bolt. To do this, you first find the angle strike leg which has holes in it. Slip that leg behind the knob end of the bolt. When you have the angle strike positioned so the lever edge is touching the curved strike, punch the screw holes and drive the screws.

Return this mechanism to its location on the frame, inserting the bolt in its guides as you do so. The operation of the lever, bolt and ratchet teeth will be obvious at this point. Next, secure the far end of the lever by making a hinge of the remaining flat strike. Position it at the lever's far end so that one screw hole is on the face of the lever and the other is on the 2″ x 4″. Slip a match between the lever and the 2″ x 4″. Punch the holes (don't drill) and drive two 1″ No. 4 flat head wood screws into these holes. Do not drive the screws tight since this is the hinge point and must be loose enough to move around. Remove the match and congratulate yourself. You have just completed cloth and warp beam installation!

8. BEATER BUILDING.

The final major assembly is the beater frame. You start this by building up the horizontal members. First locate the three pieces of door stop measuring forty-eight and forty-seven inches and four pieces of screen stock measuring forty-eight and fifty-two and one-half inches, respectively. Make a mark two inches from one end across both forty-eight inch door stops and then mark off every four inches after that for a total of twelve marks on each stop. On these lines, mark a point three-eights inches in from each edge, alternating edges.

After the marking has been completed, tape the two forty-eight inch door stops to the two forty-eight inch screen stock members. Apply tape to the edges like the binding on a book to keep the stop lined up with the screen stock. One edge of the other side of the stop will not line up with the screen stock edge. This *lip* will form the bottom of the groove for the reed to fit into. The stop will probably be slightly warped, so compensate for this by pulling it into place with tape. Drill and countersink twelve, 7/64" holes on each stop as marked to receive 1" No. 4 flat head screws. Drill through the stop only. You can tell when the drill breaks through by pressing your finger to the joint. The stop will move when the drill has broken through.

Now, drill approximately one-half inch into the screen stock with the 5/64" bit. After all twenty-four holes are completed, remove the tape, but be sure not to get the pieces mixed up. Lay a dozen one-quarter inch washers on each screen stock member so that the screw holes peek through the washer eyes. Twist all the one inch screws through, exposing their points on the underside. Carefully lay each stop on its screen stock counterpart and drive in the two end screws on each. Check to see that no washer has slipped out of place and then finish driving the rest of the screws.

Now, take the two 52-1/2" lengths of screen stock and make a mark on each 3-3/4" from one end. Then draw nine marks five inches apart starting from the 3-3/4" mark. Mark in three-quarters inches from one edge at each of these marks. Tape the already built-up part to the 52-1/2" length you just finished so that the two parts form a groove. Do this so the marks three-quarters inches in from the edge are near the flush side and not on the groove side. The *ears* or ends of the 52-1/2" stock need to protrude 2-1/4" on each side. After the lengths are positioned correctly and taped together, drill them at the marks to receive ten No. 4 flat head screws 1-1/4" long. Use 7/64" and 5/64" bits and don't forget to countersink. Drive the screws to secure the two pieces and strip them of the tape.

Select one of the two pieces you have just completed to carry the shuttle race. The remaining stop forty-seven inches long will become the race to be attached to the piece you have just selected. Mark the screw holes three-eights inches in from the square edge of the stop. Have the rounded edge face up on the same side as the marks. Start locating the holes by making a mark two inches from one end and then mark off seven inches successively until you have a total of seven points three-eights inches in from the edge. Drill and countersink these marks for 1" No. 4 screws.

Now, mark one-half inch in from one end on the forty-seven inch length of stock on the piece you selected to carry the race. Line the end of the race up with this one-half inch mark and you are ready to begin drilling holes in the built up piece so you can fasten the race onto it. If the race is warped (and it probably is), begin drilling on the end where you made the one-half inch mark and drive in a one inch screw. Proceed straightening and driving one inch screws from this end. When this is all done, haul out the sandpaper and sand where necessary, but not in the grooves.

Lay this aside and gather together the last six pieces of screen stock left in your lumber pile. These are the beater legs. Separate the pieces into groups of three with one short piece in each group. Mark ten inches from one end of the 37-1/2" piece. Place the 26-5/16" piece on the short member to make a sandwich. Mark ten inches from the end on the edge of this long piece and line it up with the short member's end. The structure should now have a ten inch deep slot, formed by the sandwich of long and short pieces.

Line everything up and put your knee on the pile to hold it steady. Mark eleven inches from the fork end to the center of the top piece and drill a quarter inch hole through all three pieces at this point. Insert a 1/4" – 2-1/2" long carriage bolt through the hole. Apply a washer and nut to the threads and tighten. Straighten everything out again, and mark two points from the opposite end. One point should be 2-1/2" from the end and the other five inches. Both marks should be at the center of the piece. Drill these two holes with a quarter inch drill and insert the 1/4" – 2-1/2" carriage bolts. Put on the washers and nuts and tighten.

Now go to the fork end and mark a point in the center one inch from the end on both prongs. Drill both with a quarter inch drill. The holes will later receive 1/4" – 3" carriage bolts. Repeat the same operations for the other group of long and short pieces. Sand as necessary.

Having completed all the members, you are now ready to assemble the frame. Insert a 5/8" – 4" machine bolt in the holes you drilled earlier in the bottom rail on the loom frame. Thread the nut on just enough to expose the bolt on the inside. Place the fork members on these bolts with the ten inch slot at the top and the bolt heads facing the weaver. Slip the assembly with the shuttle race into the slots of both forks. The race must face the weaver. Press the horizontal piece down to the bottom of the slot.

If your reed has arrived, you should install it now. Place one side of the reed in the groove of the beater frame. Then insert the top beater bar with the exception that the groove on this one faces down to capture the reed. You now install the 1/4" – 3" carriage bolts through the holes you drilled one inch from the top of the beater uprights. Put on the wing nuts.

Stand back and admire your loom. There are only three more items to be completed and you will be ready to weave. First you need to stain and/or varnish the beater frame and then make the apron and crank.

9. APRON AND CRANK CREATION.

When you have had time to puff up with pride, long enough to let the finish dry on the beater frame, begin to make the crank. First study Illustration 19 to get the general idea.

The crank handle is made by drilling a 5/16'' hole in the warp beam full round sticking out the right side of the loom. Thread a nut 1-1/2'' from the end of the only 5/16'' eye bolt left. Slip on a washer and the remaining nut on the other side and tighten. Move the *lollipop* end of the bolt so it is parallel with the face of the 2'' x 4''. Drill the end of the four inch dowel in that rapidly vanishing lumber pile so it will receive the remaining 3/4'' No. 4 round head screw. Mount a rivet burr, the one-fourth inch and three-eights inch washer on the screw and drive the screw in the end of the dowel. Adjust the washers before finally tightening. Slide the dowel through the bolt eye. The whole process is shown in Illustration 19.

Next, capture the dowel by wrapping fourteen or so turns of one-eighth inch nylon cord around it. Use about ten and one-half feet of cord. The wrapping, which is demonstrated in Illustration 19, is called seizing and the type of seizing is called French or grapevine seizing. Start the seizing by wrapping a loop around the dowel and tucking the end around and underneath the standing part of the rope. Continue to wrap the dowel one turn at a time and slip the end under the rope from the inside and pull tight to form a hitch. Wrap again and form another hitch, continuing this process for a dozen or so turns. Finish it off with an overhand knot at the last hitch. Keep pressing the seizing against the eye bolt as you go. This seizing will loosen during use and should be glued in place.

Fabricate the aprons for the beams by turning in nine eye screws on both the cloth and warp beams. Locate the eyes one-half inch in from the edge of the 1'' x 4'' on the wide face. Start one-half inch in from the edge opposite the ratchet and mark off eight five inch spaces. Drill these points and install the screw eyes on both beams. Cut two forty-three foot lengths of one-eighth inch nylon cord. Start from one end of the cloth beam and run the length of one of the cords through all the eyes on that beam. Do the same for the warp beam and then tie off each end of the cords with a figure eight knot like the knots you used on the roller system.

You now have forty-three feet of nylon cord knotted at both ends and strung through the screw eyes on both beams. Most of this length of cord is hanging out one end, and your task now is to pull up the slack into loops between each eye until the entire length of each cord is pulled up. Tie off and adjust the loops to hang at approximately the same level. You will use the same knot to install the apron bars as you used for the treadle tie-up earlier.

The apron bars are the two sticks of wood called the parting stop measuring 1/2'' x 3/4'' x 41''. Sand these bars to knock off the sharp edges. If you wish, varnish or finish them before installing. Begin installing one bar at one end of the loops you just pulled through on the cloth beam. Lay the loop, called the *bright,* back against the standing part of the cord. This forms two holes for the apron bar to pass through. Level the bar by *plucking* the cord while applying strain to the bar. The knot you are using is called a switch, lark's head or cow hitch and it is shown in Illustration 19. Now, lead the apron around the breast beam from the top of the cloth beam. Follow the same procedure to install the second bar and then lead the warp apron (the bar and rope apparatus you just completed) around the back beam from the bottom of the warp beam.

A final congratulations — you have just completed your loom. After weeks of confusion and apprehension, it is done. If you are a complete neophyte, however, you are about to launch another series of traumas in learning how to *dress* and use your new loom to make cloth. At any rate, at this point, you can still sit back and admire your work and say, *This I have done.* You can say the same thing, in fact, even if you aren't a neophyte.

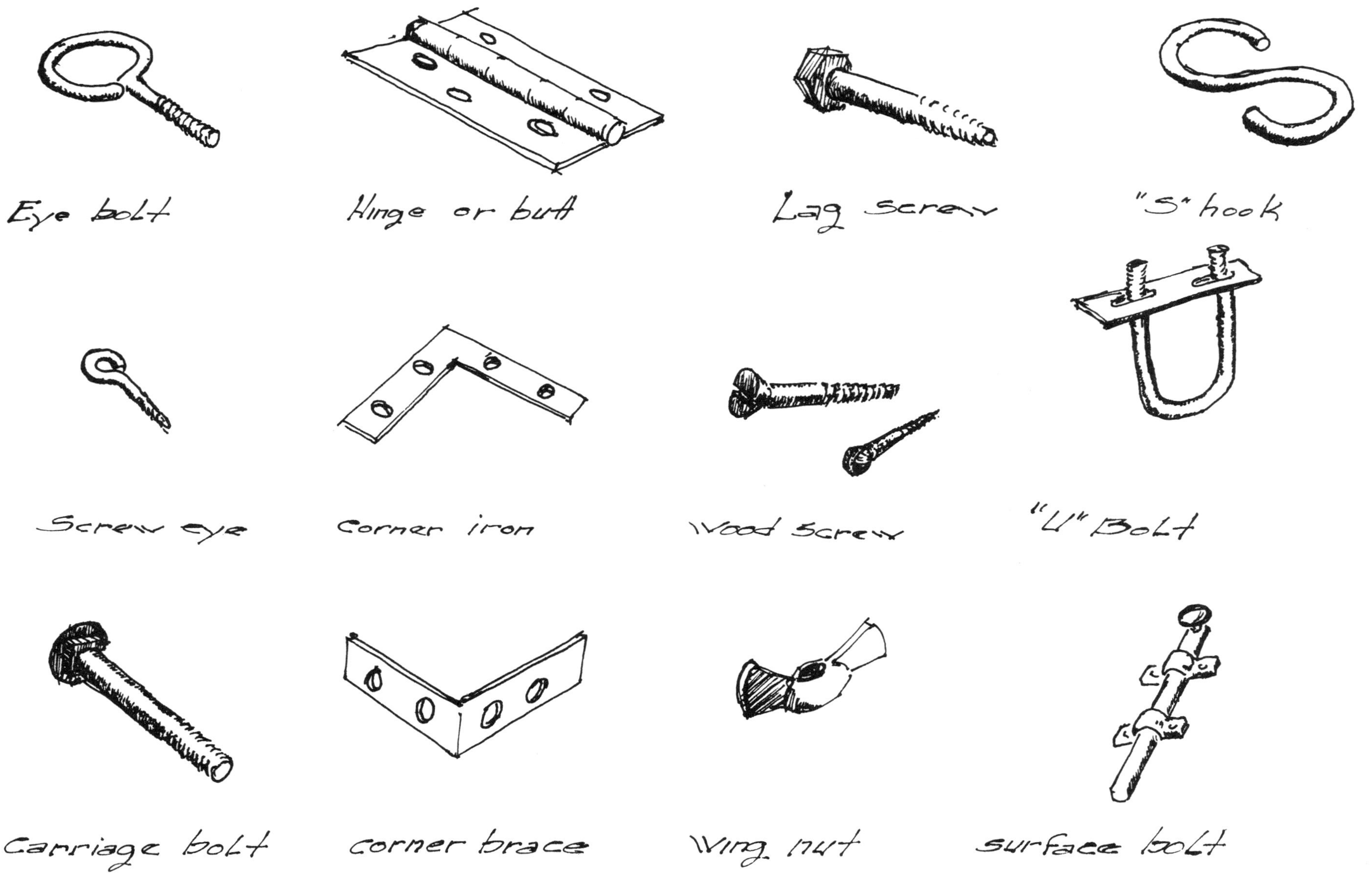

"S" hook

"U" Bolt

Surface bolt

Lag Screw

Wood Screw

Wing nut

Hinge or butt

Corner iron

Corner brace

Eye bolt

Screw Eye

Carriage bolt

ILLUSTRATION 1 – LOOM HARDWARE

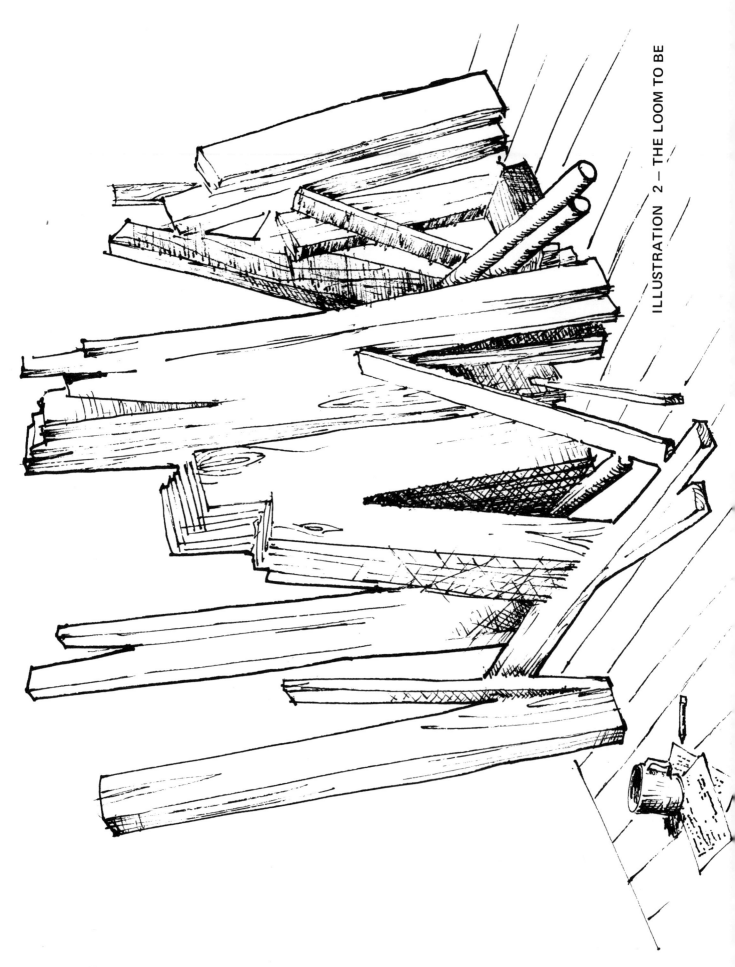

ILLUSTRATION 2 — THE LOOM TO BE

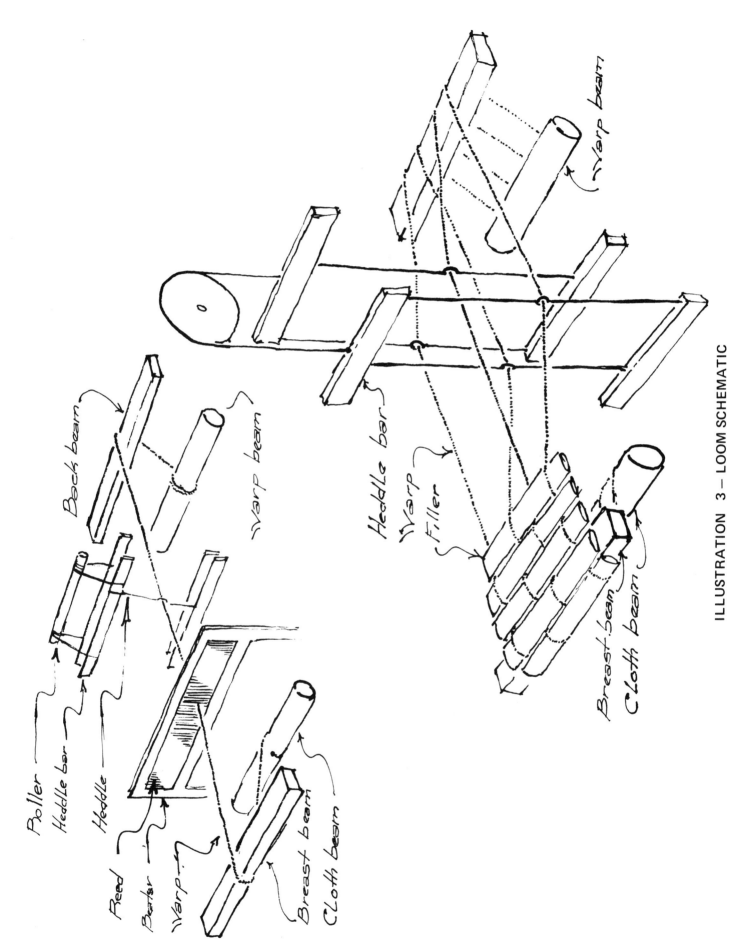

Back beam

Warp beam

Roller
Heddle bar

Heddle

Reed

Beater

Warp

Breast beam
Cloth beam

Heddle bar

Warp
Filler

Warp beam

Breast beam
Cloth beam

ILLUSTRATION 3 – LOOM SCHEMATIC

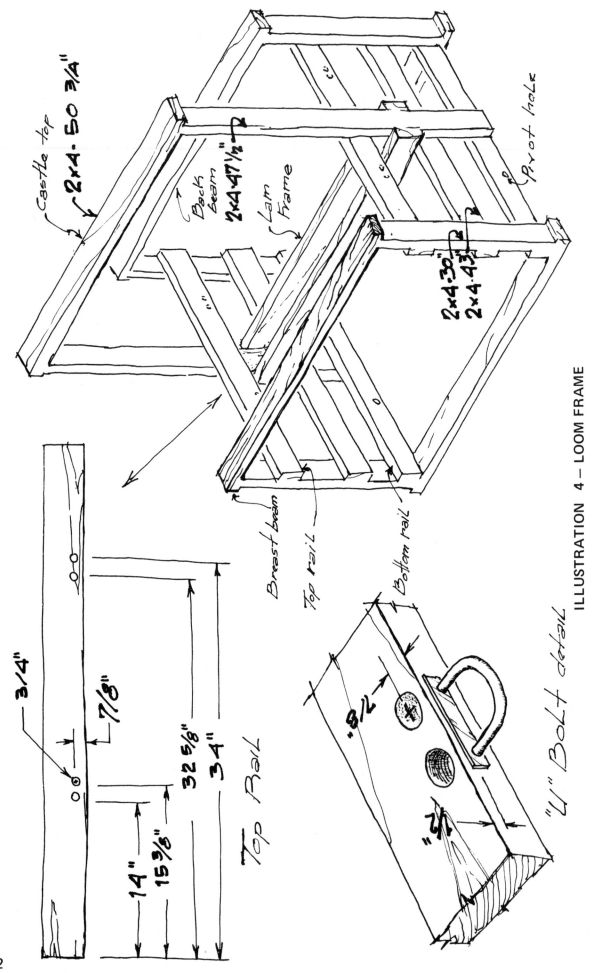

Castle top

2×4 - 50 3/4"

Back beam
2×4 47½"

Lam Frame

Pivot hole

2×4 - 30"
2×4 - 43"

Breast beam

Top rail

Bottom rail

Top Rail

3/4"

7/8"

32 5/8"

34"

14"

15 5/8"

"U" Bolt detail

1/2"

1/2"

42

ILLUSTRATION 4 — LOOM FRAME

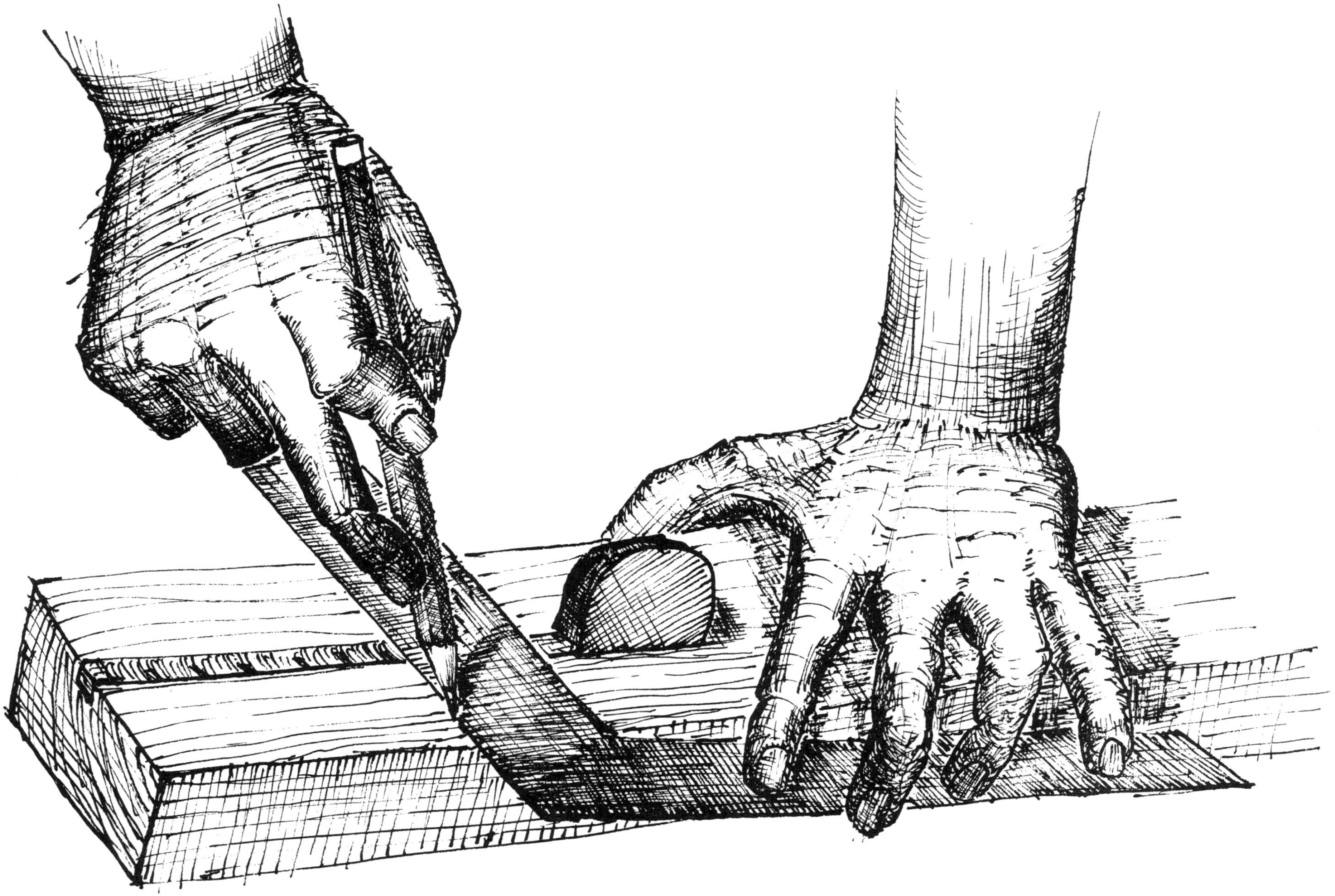

ILLUSTRATION 5 — USING CARPENTER'S SQUARE AND TAPE MEASURE

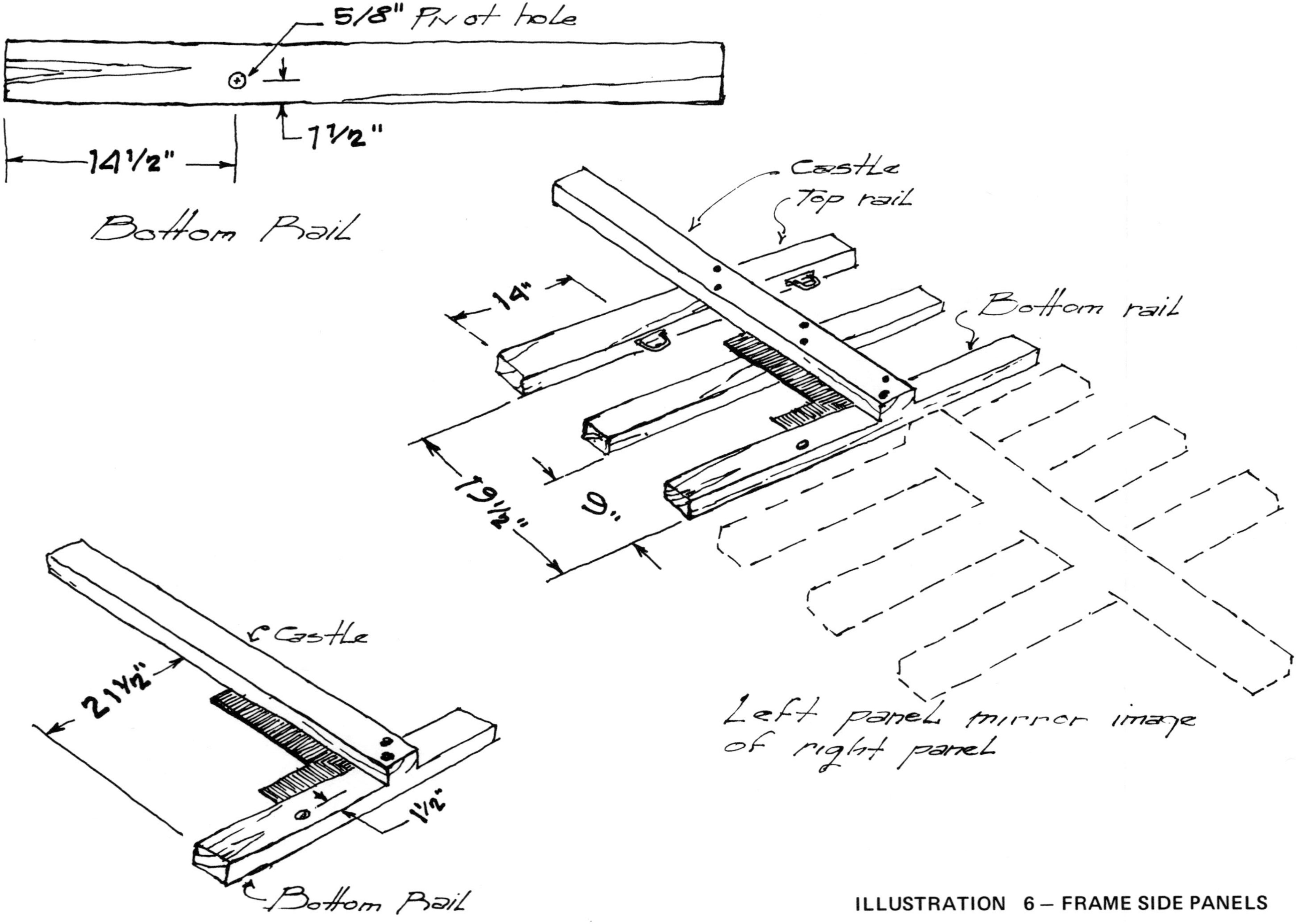

Bottom rail

Castle
Top rail

Left panel mirror image
of right panel

9"

19½"

1"

5/8" Pivot hole

1½"

14½"

Bottom Rail

Castle

Bottom Rail

1½"

21¼"

44

ILLUSTRATION 6 – FRAME SIDE PANELS

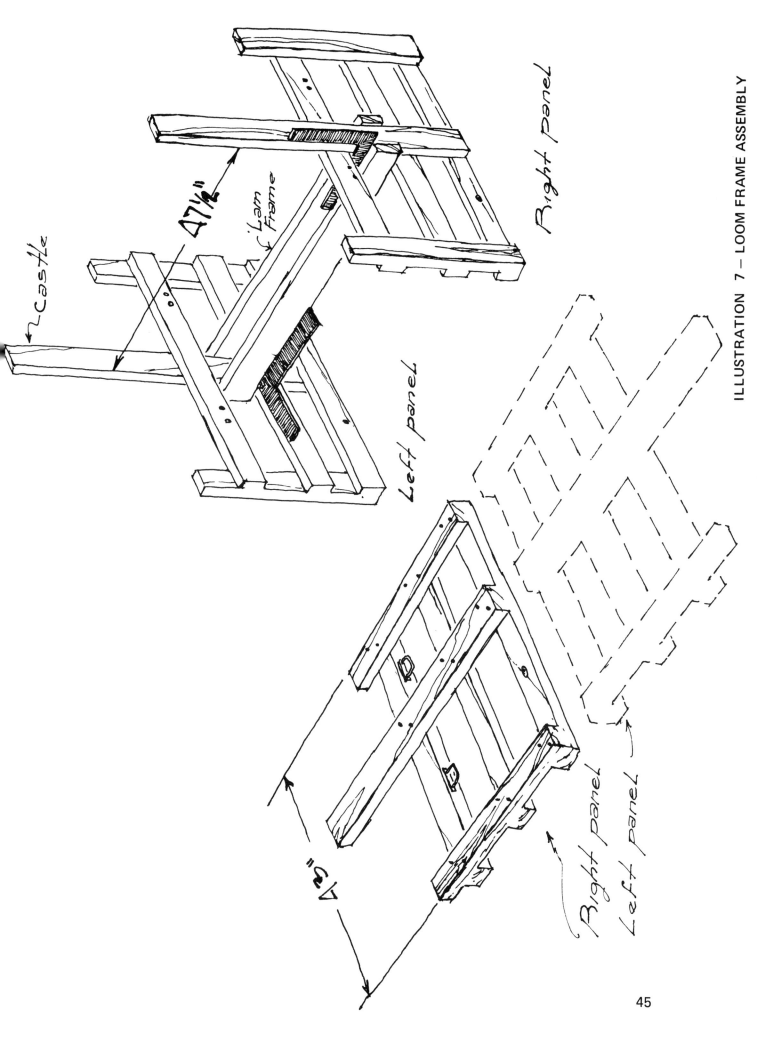

Castle

47½"

Lam Frame

Left panel

Right panel

42"

Right panel

Left panel

ILLUSTRATION 7 – LOOM FRAME ASSEMBLY

Breast beam
Half surface butt
Upright

Detail @ Breast beam

47½"

Castle
Top rail

Drill thru both beams - ¼"

1¾"

Llam frame

To line up with 2×4

Bottom rail

Floor

Detail @ Left Side of Loom

ILLUSTRATION 8 – FRAME DETAILS

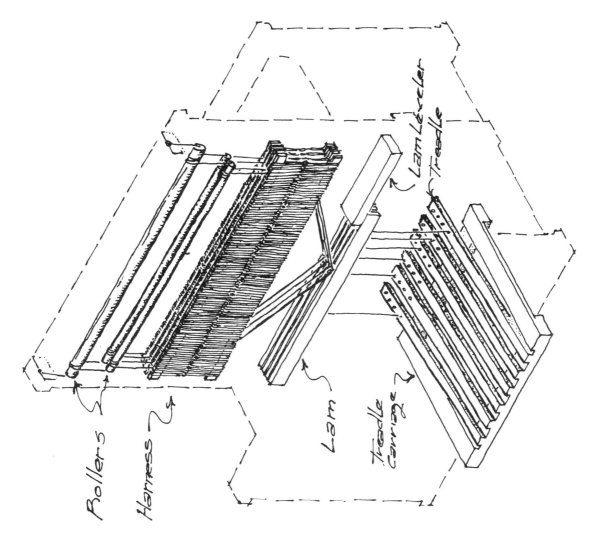

Rollers

Harness

Lam

Treadle Carriage

Lam Leveler

Treadle

ILLUSTRATION 9 – HARNESS SYSTEM

47

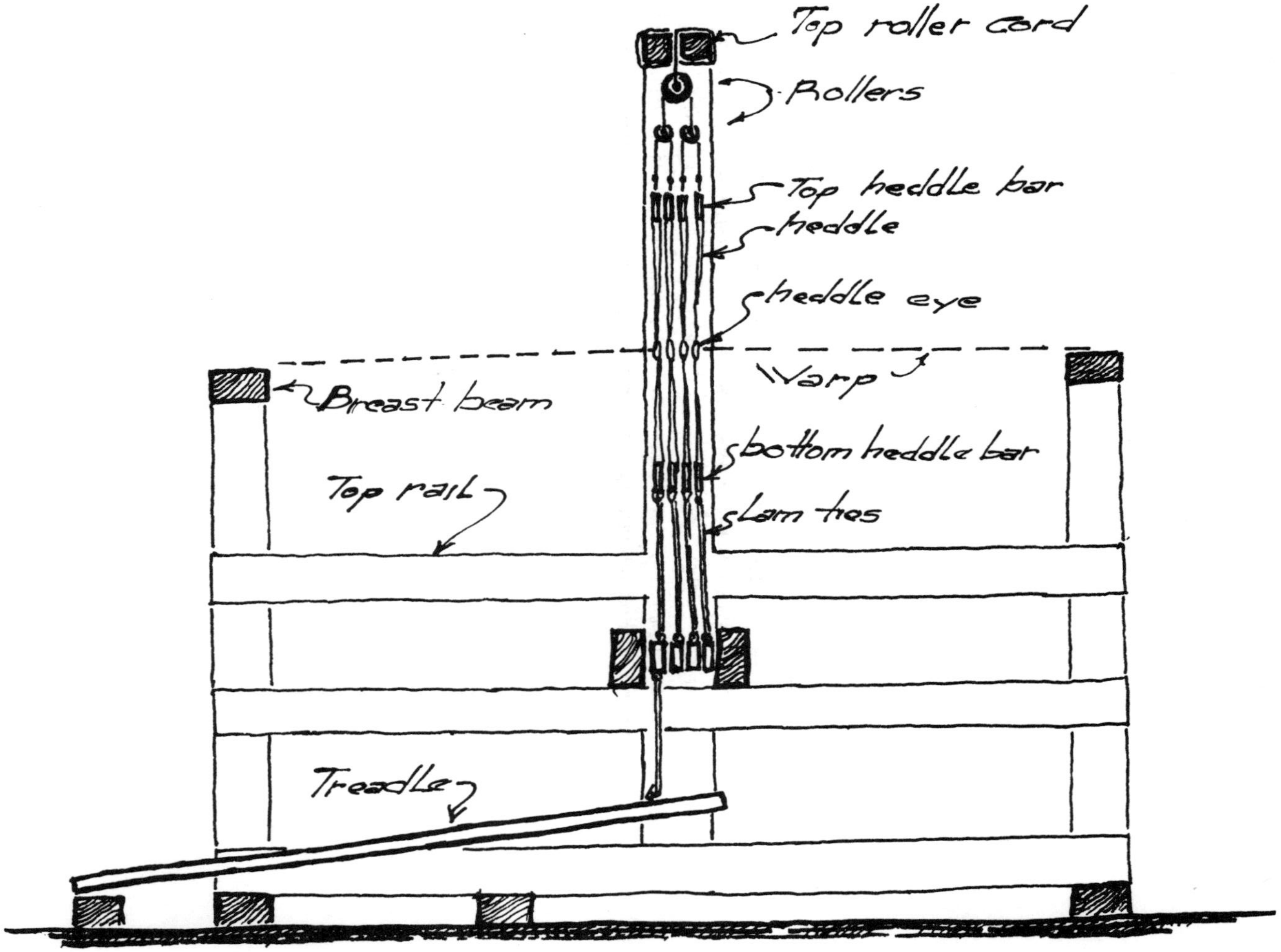

ILLUSTRATION 10 – COUNTERBALANCE SYSTEM

Top roller cord

Rollers

Top heddle bar

heddle

heddle eye

Warp

bottom heddle bar

lam ties

Breast beam

Top rail

Treadle

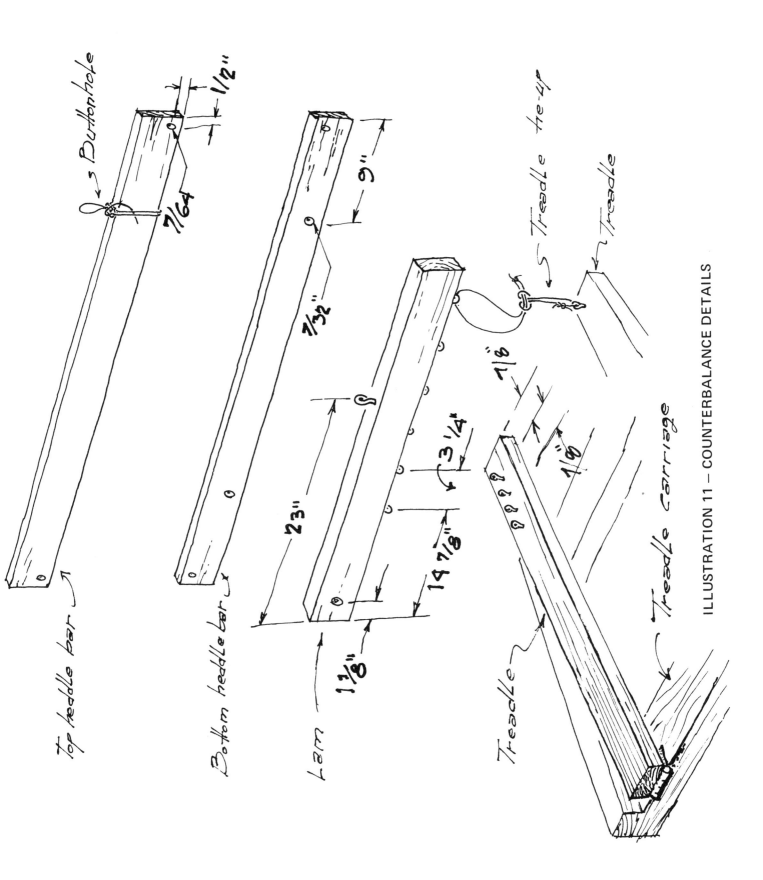

Top heddle bar

Buttonhole

1/2"

7/64

Bottom heddle bar

9"

7/32

23"

3 1/4"

14 7/8"

1 3/8"

Lam

Treadle tie-up

Treadle

3/8"

1/40

Treadle

Treadle Carriage

ILLUSTRATION 11 – COUNTERBALANCE DETAILS

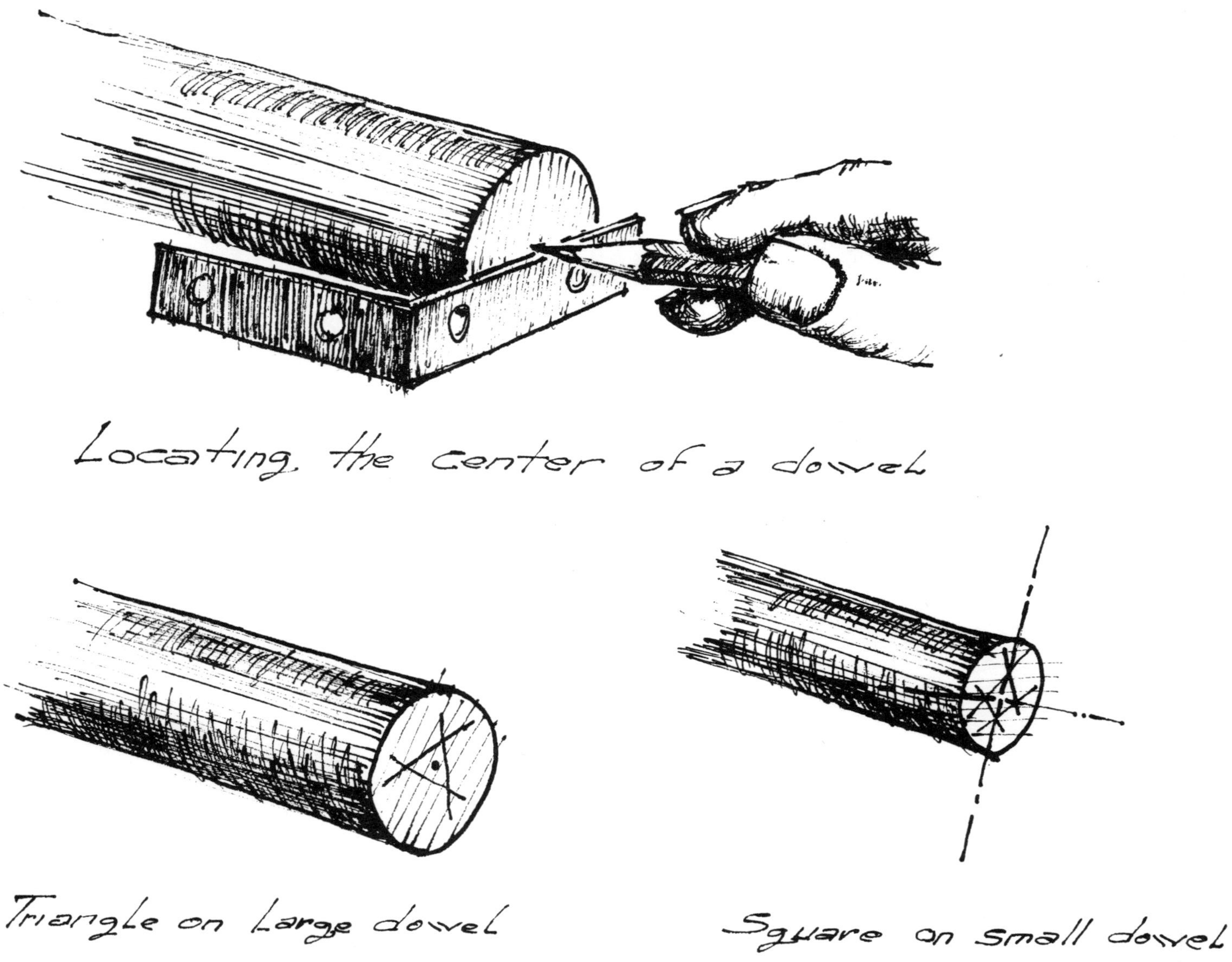

Locating the Center of a dowel

Square on Small dowel

Triangle on Large dowel

ILLUSTRATION 12 — LOCATING THE CENTER OF A DOWEL

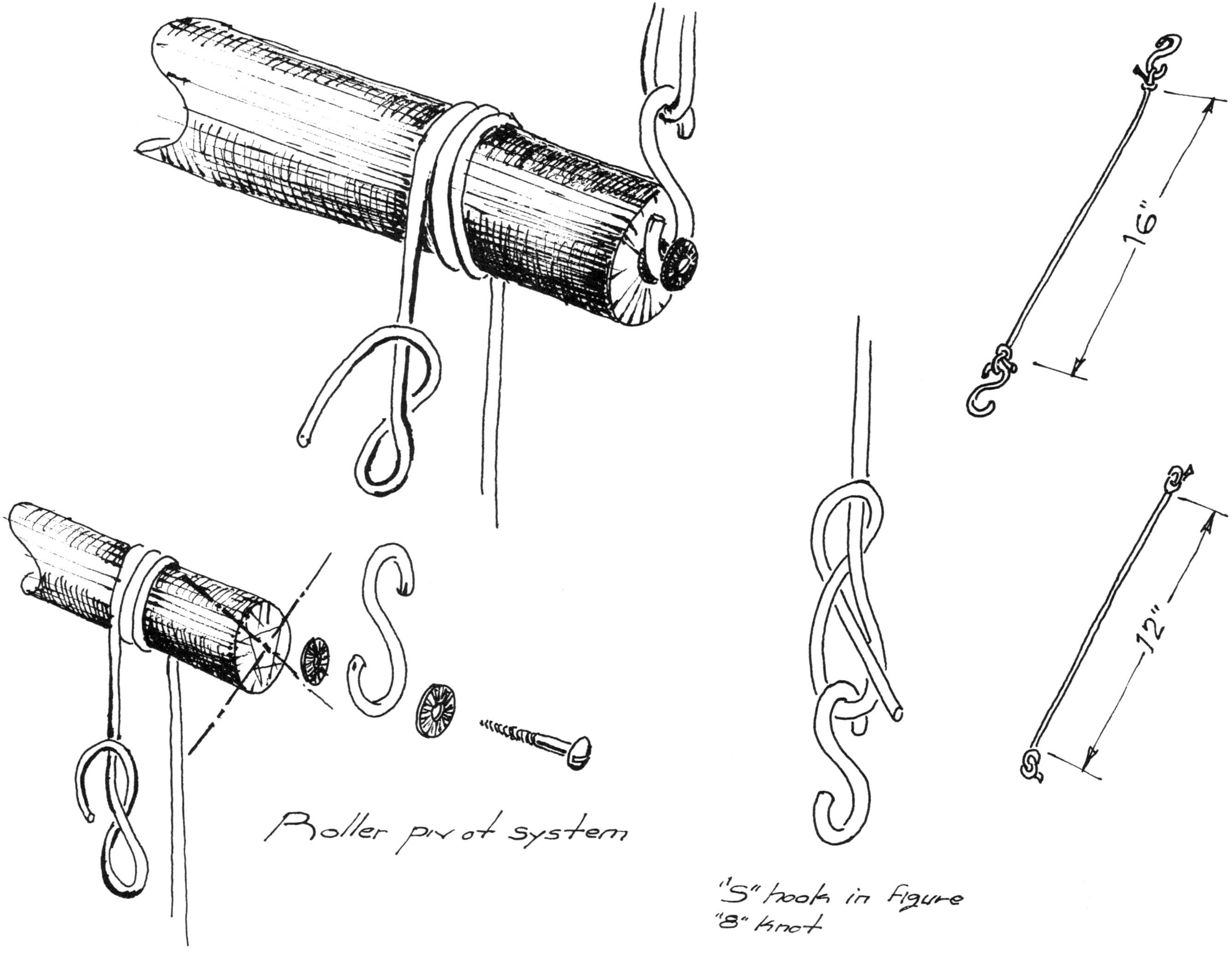

16"

12"

"S" hook in Figure
"8" knot

Roller Pivot System

ILLUSTRATION 13 — ROLLER PIVOT SYSTEM

Heddle board

11"
5½"
5¼"

Top heddle bar

3"

Top heddle bar

Heddle bar brace

Bottom heddle bar

Lam tie

½"

ILLUSTRATION 14 – HEDDLE DETAILS

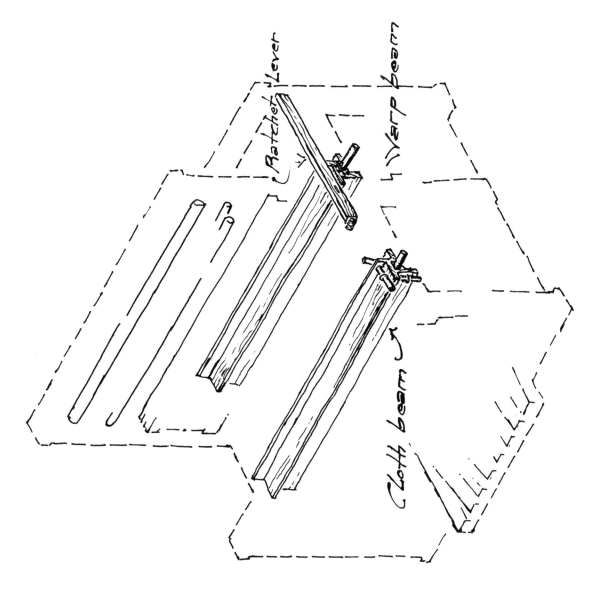

Ratchet Lever

Warp beam

Cloth beam

ILLUSTRATION 15 — WARP AND CLOTH BEAMS

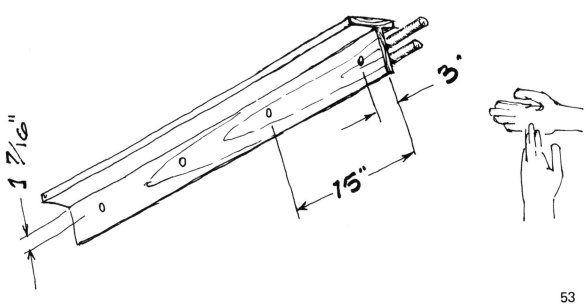

1 7/16"

3"

15"

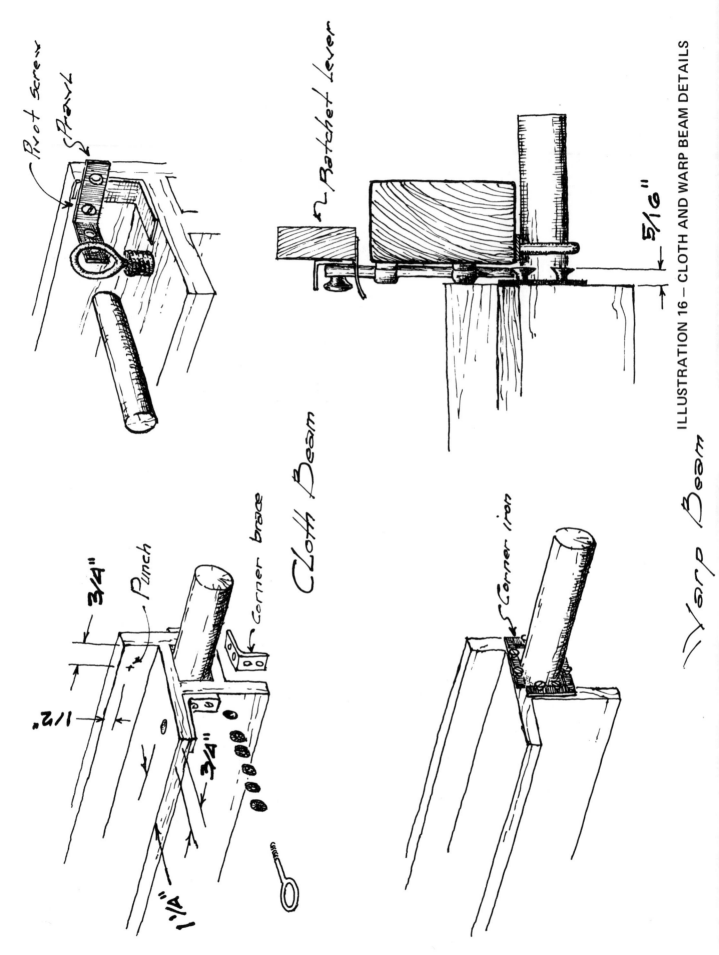

Pivot Screw
Prawl
Ratchet Lever
5/16"
Cloth Beam
Warp Beam
Corner brace
Corner iron
Punch
3/4"
1 1/2"
3/4"
1 1/4"

ILLUSTRATION 16 – CLOTH AND WARP BEAM DETAILS

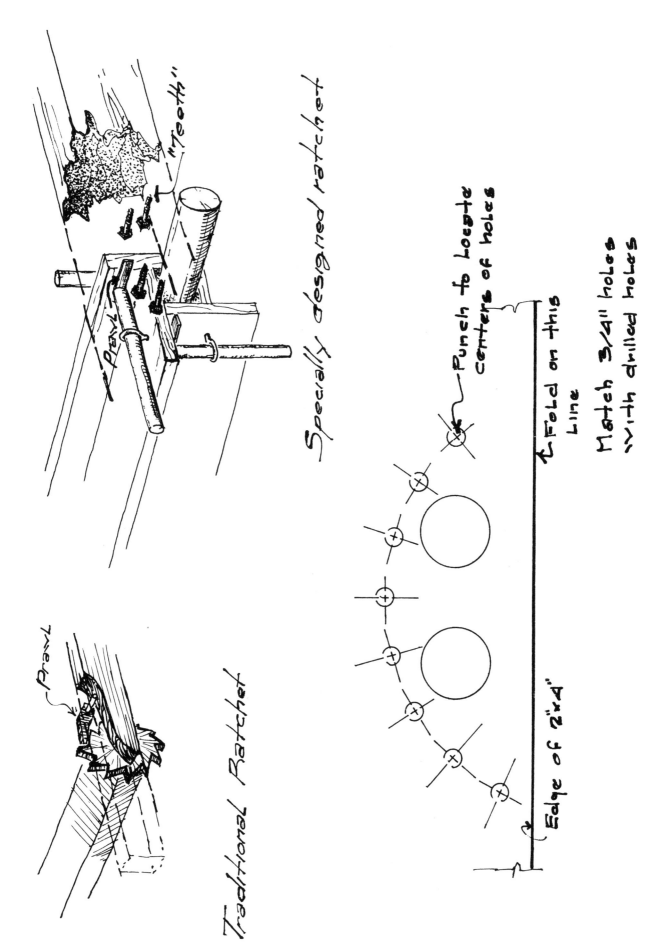

"Teeth"

Specially designed ratchet

Pawl

Traditional Ratchet

Punch to locate centers of holes

Fold on this Line

Match 3/4" holes with drilled holes

Edge of 2"x4"

ILLUSTRATION 17 – RATCHET LAYOUT

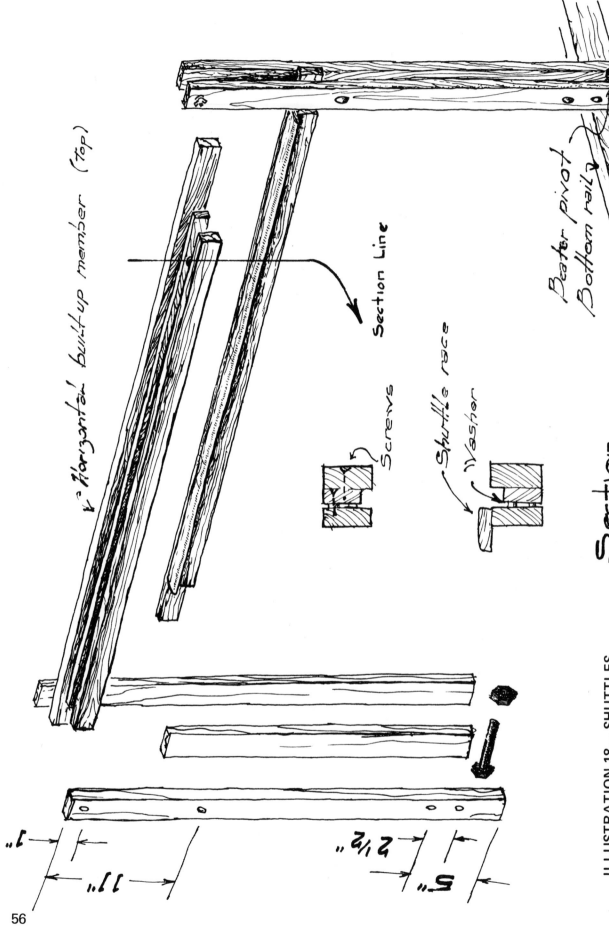

1/8" Horizontal built-up member (top)

Section Line

Screws

Shuttle race

Washer

Beater pivot

Bottom rail

Section

1"

11"

2 1/2"

5"

56

ILLUSTRATION 18 – SHUTTLES

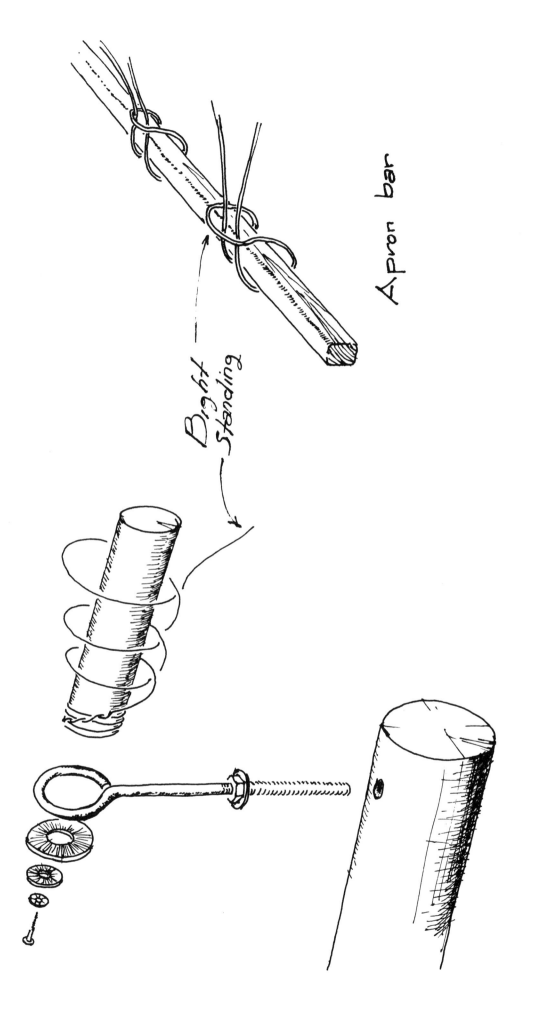

Bright
Standing

Apron bar

Crank

ILLUSTRATION 19 — CRANK AND APRON BAR

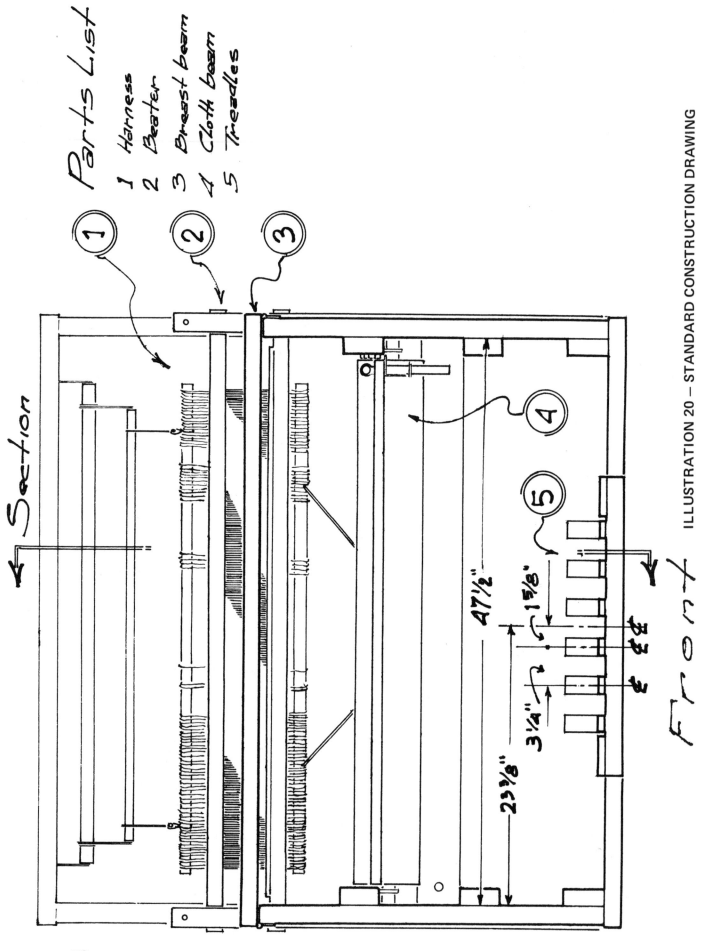

Parts List

1 Harness
2 Beater
3 Breast beam
4 Cloth beam
5 Treadles

Section

Front

ILLUSTRATION 20 – STANDARD CONSTRUCTION DRAWING

47½"

1⅝"

3¼"

23⅝"

58

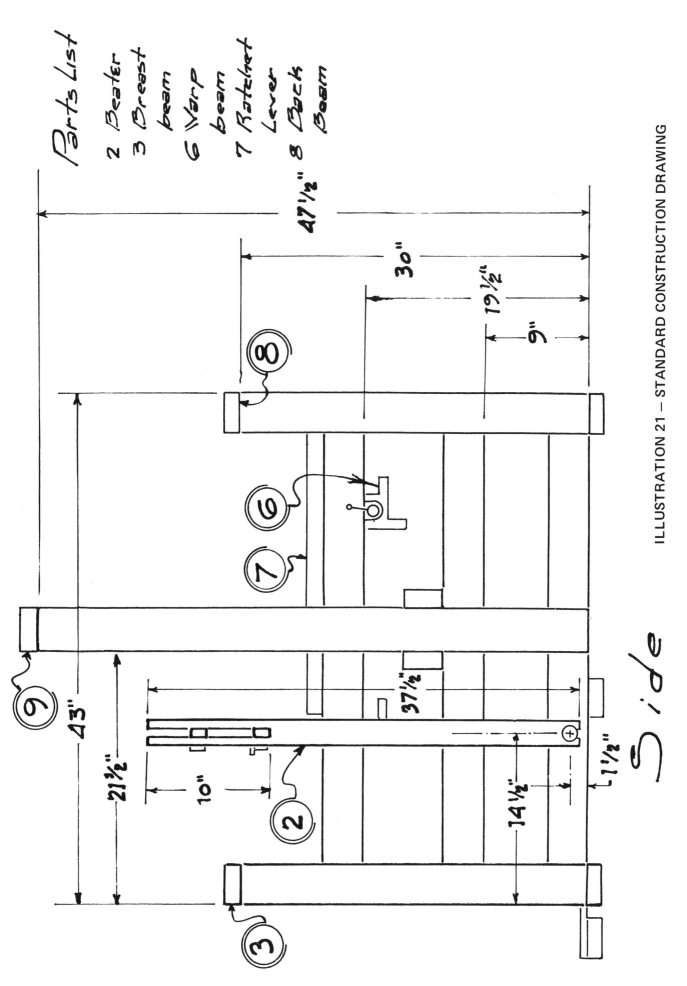

ILLUSTRATION 21 — STANDARD CONSTRUCTION DRAWING

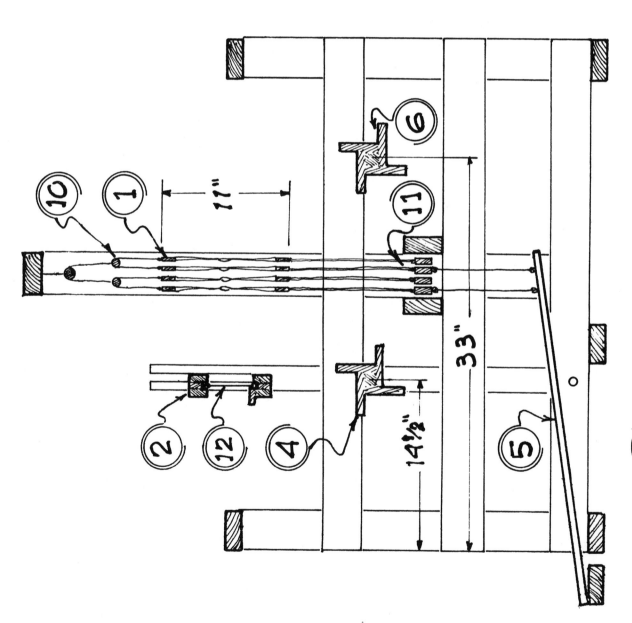

Parts List
1 Harnesses
2 Beater
4 Cloth beam
5 Treadles
6 Warp beam
10 Roller
11 Lams
12 Reed

Section

ILLUSTRATION 22 — STANDARD CONSTRUCTION DRAWING

60

GLOSSARY

Apron — the element, canvas or cord, which connects the apron bar to both the cloth and warp beams

Apron Bar — a bar to which the warp is tied on both cloth and warp beams

Back Beam — sometimes called whip roll, the beam at the back of a loom over which the warp passes

Beater — the framework which a weaver grabs and pulls forward to press the filler or weft into place in the warp while weaving

Bight — the term used to describe a loop in a length of rope

Breast Beam — Beam at the front of the loom over which the cloth moves as it is being woven

Buttons and Buttonholes — terms used exclusively in this book to identify the links between the rollers and top heddle bars

Castle — framework on loom which supports the harness mechanism

Castle Side — side member of castle frame

Castle Top — top member of castle frame

Cloth Beam — a beam which stores cloth while it is being woven

Counterbalance — a type of loom. Refers to the method of moving the harnesses

Crank — that part of the loom which one turns to wind the warp onto the warp beam; also a person who hasn't had enough sleep

Dent or Dent Count — the number of spaces in a reed between teeth in one inch, i.e. an 8 dent reed has 8 spaces per inch

Dog — a loose tooth that prevents the ratchet from moving and holds the warp in tension

Frame — the cage within which all the loom parts are located

Harnesses — the elements which spread the warp so a filler can be passed through to make cloth, including heddle bar braces, heddle bars and heddles

Heddle — that element in the harness which holds the warp

Heddle Bar — there are both top and bottom heddle bars; the top heddle bar supports the upper end of the heddles, while the bottom heddle bar holds the bottom ends of the heddles

Heddle Bar Brace — term used only in this book and the thing that holds the ends of the heddle bars

Heddle Board — a board with nails in it which is used to hold heddle making material in place while heddles are being made

Heddle Eye — the hole in the heddle through which the warp passes

Lam Frame — as opposed to the loom frame, the lam frame is within the loom frame and holds the lams

Lam Leveler — exclusive to this book and a simple device to hold the lams level

Lam Tie — the cord used to tie the bottom heddle bar to the appropriate lam

Lams — a bar held in the lam frame through which the treadles are tied to the harnesses

Loom — an instrument or machine used to make cloth, developed long before the written word in all known cultures

Neophyte — a person who has yet to build a loom and what you won't be when you get through

Prawl — see dog

Rail — there are top and bottom rails and they are the horizontal members of the loom frame

Ratchet — the gear which determines how far the cloth is advanced during weaving

Ratchet Release — a lever which pulls the prawl out of the way of the ratchet, thus allowing either cloth or warp beam to move during weaving

Reed — the comb in the beater that presses the filler into place

Roller — the dowel mechanism which holds the harnesses and allows them to move

Shuttle Race — the flat portion of the beater frame in the front of and at the base of the reed facing the weaver and supporting the shuttle as it races across

Standing — a term used to describe that portion of rope which is not used for forming a knot

Treadle — a foot-operated lever which activates the harness mechanism through the lams

Treadle Carriage — also called treadle frame and that part of the loom which holds the treadles

Treadle Tie-Up — the cords and method by which the treadles are tied to the lams

Warp Beam — a beam which carries and stores the warp

Weaving Width — the maximum width of cloth that can be woven on a loom

NOTES